PRAISE FOR CATHY GLASS

'Poignant and revealing ... real-life stories such as these have helped to move and inspire a generation' *Sunday Mirror*

'A true tale of hope' *OK!* Magazine

'Heartbreaking' *Mirror*

'A life-affirming read ... that proves sometimes a little hope is all you need' *Heat* Magazine

'A hugely touching and emotional true tale' *Star* Magazine

'Foster carers rarely get the praise they deserve, but Cathy Glass's book should change all that' *First* Magazine

'Cannot fail to move those who read it' Adoption-net

'Once again, Cathy Glass has blown me away with a poignant story' The Writing Garnet, book blogger

'Brilliant book. I'd expect nothing less from Cathy ... I cried, of course' Goodreads review

'... gripping page-turner from start to finish ... emotive and heart-wrenching ...' Kate Hall, ok blogger

'... another great read ... no complex narrative, just pure storytelling ...' 5* Kindle review

'Filled with compassion and love' Victoria Goldman, Lovereading

'Never disappoints and brings a tear to my eye' Hannah, book blogger

'Simply yet eloquently told ... Cathy's years of fostering experience shine a beam of light across the pages'

Liz Robinson, Lovereading

'Amazing writing from an incredible lady'

5* Amazon review

'Wonderfully written book' 5* Kindle review

'A captivating insight into the life of a foster carer'

Victoria Goldman, Lovereading

'I have read all Cathy Glass's books and none disappoint'

5* Amazon review

'Great job, Cathy Glass. Keep doing what you do and I'll keep reading' Goodreads review

No One to Miss Me

ALSO BY CATHY GLASS

FOSTERING MEMOIRS

Cut
The Silent Cry
Daddy's Little Princess
Nobody's Son
Cruel to be Kind
The Night the Angels Came
A Long Way from Home
A Baby's Cry
The Saddest Girl in the World
Please Don't Take My Baby
Will You Love Me?
I Miss Mummy
Saving Danny
Girl Alone
Where Has Mummy Gone?
Damaged
Hidden
Mummy Told Me Not to Tell
Another Forgotten Child
The Child Bride
Can I Let You Go?
Finding Stevie
Innocent
Too Scared to Tell
A Terrible Secret
A Life Lost
An Innocent Baby
Neglected
A Family Torn Apart
Unwanted
Unsafe
Helpless

INSPIRED BY EXPERIENCE

The Girl in the Mirror
My Dad's a Policeman
Run, Mummy, Run

SHARING HER EXPERTISE

Happy Kids
Happy Adults
Happy Mealtimes for Kids
About Writing and How to Publish

WRITING AS LISA STONE

The Darkness Within
Stalker
The Doctor
Taken
The Cottage
The Gathering
The Murder Room
The Forever House

THE MULTI-MILLION-COPY BESTSELLING AUTHOR

CATHY GLASS

No One to Miss Me

Can Cathy help troubled Lily sort her life out and piece together the truth?

HARPER element

Certain details in this story, including names, places and dates, have been changed to protect the family's privacy.

HarperElement
An imprint of HarperCollins*Publishers*
1 London Bridge Street
London SE1 9GF

www.harpercollins.co.uk

HarperCollins*Publishers*
Macken House, 39/40 Mayor Street Upper
Dublin 1, D01 C9W8, Ireland

First published by HarperElement 2026

1 3 5 7 9 10 8 6 4 2

A catalogue record of this book is available from the British Library

ISBN 978-0-00-880321-6

Printed and bound in the UK using 100% renewable electricity at CPI Group (UK) Ltd

FSC www.fsc.org
MIX
Paper | Supporting responsible forestry
FSC® C013604

ACKNOWLEDGEMENTS

A big thank-you to my family; my editors, Ajda and Holly; my literary agent, Andrew; my UK publisher HarperCollins, and my overseas publishers, who are now too numerous to list by name. Last, but definitely not least, a big thank-you to my readers for your unfailing support and kind words. They are much appreciated.

AUTHOR'S NOTE

Suicide now accounts for 1 per cent of all deaths globally (World Health Organization).

CHAPTER ONE

AFTER MIDNIGHT

It was near midnight on Boxing Day, the day after Christmas. I'd said goodbye to my guests – namely family and a few close friends – and had got into bed, exhausted. Paula, my youngest daughter, who was in her early thirties, was getting into bed too. I could hear her moving around. We'd said goodnight and that we'd see each other when we woke in the morning, whenever that was. She was planning on a lie-in and so was I.

I'd snuggled down into bed and switched off my bedside light. It was great having family over at Christmas but very tiring. Tomorrow would be a more relaxing day. I had nothing planned. My eyes closed and I was just nodding off, thinking about the wonderful time we'd all had, when I heard a loud bang come from outside the front of my house. My bedroom is over the porch, so I sometimes hear people who've had too much to drink wandering down the road, laughing and joking, especially at that time of year. I listened, expecting to hear voices, but it remained quiet outside. What was it? I vaguely wondered. I wasn't scared. I'd lived as the only adult in my house for many years – since my husband had left me when my children were little. I'd never had a break-in yet, apart from a foster child many years ago.

I listened for a while but the sound wasn't repeated. I turned over and was just dropping off to sleep when I heard a loud crash. I immediately sat up in bed. It had definitely come from the front of the house beneath where my bedroom was, and it sounded as though it had come from the porch. I switched on my bedside lamp, then got out of bed. My heart was starting to beat loudly. I went to the curtains, parted them, and looked out. I could see the streetlamp in front of the house but no people. I continued to look for a few minutes. The porch was directly underneath my bedroom window, so I couldn't see that.

What should I do? I wondered. Perhaps it was a large cat or a fox? But it didn't sound like that. It sounded human. It was a loud smash. I put on my dressing gown and went out onto the landing. Paula's bedroom door was opening too.

'Did you hear that, Mum?' she asked.

'Yes, I did. What on earth was it?'

We went to the top of the stairs and listened. We couldn't hear anything. I could see Paula was spooked, and to some degree I was too. We stayed there, waiting and listening. A scraping sound came from the doorstep.

'Shall we call the police?' Paula asked.

'Not yet. I'm going to open the door on the chain. It sounds as though someone is in the porch. They won't be able to get in.'

'Be careful,' she warned.

We went slowly downstairs, Paula a little behind me, to the front door. The Christmas decorations stirred as we passed them. I never normally use the front-door chain, but now I put it into place and, with my heart racing, I gradually opened the door a little. I couldn't see anyone.

'Who's there?' I asked, my hand on the door.

'Lily,' a small voice returned. 'Can I come in?'

'I'm sorry, I don't know a Lily. Have you got the right address?' I still couldn't see her.

'Yes. You're Cathy Glass, foster carer,' she said. 'I haven't anywhere to stay. You looked after me ten years ago.'

I looked at Paula, and as I did, the penny dropped.

'Is it Lily Saunders?' I asked, and opened the door to the full length of the chain. I could just see part of her face.

'Yes.'

'What on earth are you doing here?' I asked, removing the chain from the door.

I wouldn't have recognized her if she hadn't said who she was. It was too long ago. I looked at the shattered pot in the porch.

'Sorry,' she said.

'You'd better come in. It's freezing out there.'

She was wearing a thin denim jacket, a cotton shirt and trousers. Her teeth were chattering.

'Come through,' I said, and closed the front door behind her.

We went down the hall and into the living room at the back of the house, where I switched on the light. I could hear our cat, Sheba, scratching to be let out of the kitchen.

'Sit down,' I told Lily.

'Thank you. I'm sorry I woke you. I didn't know where else to go. I was going to sleep in your porch.'

I looked at her. 'Do you want a hot drink?' I asked.

'Yes. Hot chocolate, like you used to make.'

I was astounded. As far as I could remember, Lily had only been with us for two weeks on respite fostering nearly ten years ago, when she'd been eight, before going for adoption. But I did seem to remember that she liked her hot chocolate. Foster carers remember these details.

I went out of the living room, leaving Paula standing there in the centre of the room, staring at her. I heard Lily say, 'You've changed.'

I opened the kitchen door and Sheba shot out into the living room. As far as I could remember Lily liked cats. I made the hot chocolate and returned.

'Do you want to go to bed?' I asked Paula.

'No, I'll stay here with you.'

She sat on the sofa a little way from Lily. I handed Lily her hot chocolate.

'So, you're eighteen now?' I asked, sitting in the armchair.

'Yes. Can I have a biscuit, please? I haven't eaten.'

'Do you want a sandwich instead?'

'Yes.'

'Cheese, ham or turkey?'

'Cheese, please.'

'Do you want anything, Paula?' I asked her.

'No, thank you.'

I left Lily gently stroking Sheba, who had replaced Sammy when he'd died. Sheba was a rescue cat who was five years old. She was black with a white mark on her face, and had eventually settled in. She was quite feral to begin with but had now calmed down. I made the cheese sandwich and put it on a plate with a packet of crisps. The poor girl looked like she could do with a good meal. I carried it through to the living room. She was still stroking Sheba. She and Paula weren't talking. She took the plate and immediately began eating ravenously and drinking the hot chocolate. She didn't stop until she'd finished. Paula and I sat there and waited.

'So, what have you been doing to come here tonight?' I asked her.

'You're the only other person I know down here,' she said.

I thought what a large part foster carers play in these children's lives. She was with us such a short time, and it was ten years ago, and yet she still remembered me.

'Who did you come to see?' I asked.

She didn't answer.

'I'm not doing full-time fostering any more,' I said, wanting to get that out of the way. 'I do respite and some outreach work. I have grandchildren now.'

'Can I stay tonight?' she asked. 'I'll find somewhere tomorrow.'

'You can, but isn't someone expecting you home?'

'Not really.'

'You were adopted as far as I remember.'

'It didn't work out,' she said sadly.

'Oh dear. So, who have you been living with?' I asked. Someone must be missing her, I thought.

'I've been living in a hostel.'

'We need to phone them and tell them you're safe.'

'Can you phone them? I don't like them. They'll be angry.'

'What's their telephone number?' I asked.

She gave me the phone number of Maddison's Hostel, which was over a hundred miles away.

'When did you leave there?' I asked.

'Early this morning.'

I knew there was a lot she wasn't telling me, but for now I needed to phone Maddison's Hostel and tell them Lily was safe. I imagined they were worried sick.

I called the number and left a message on their answerphone. I assumed they were all in bed and someone would listen to the message and call me when they woke.

'I think it's time we went to bed,' I said to Lily. 'Do you need pyjamas or a night dress?' She just had a small bag with her.

'Yes, please.'

'Toothbrush, toothpaste and so forth?'

She nodded. 'Sorry to be a pain.'

'You're not. We'll talk tomorrow.' I smiled. 'The small bedroom is empty. The bed is made up.'

'That's the one I used before,' she exclaimed excitedly. 'It overlooks the back garden. But you had Adrian and Lucy here too.'

Not for the first time, she took my breath away. She was right, she had stayed in that bedroom; it was the one I used for fostering. Adrian and Lucy had been here too for some of the time, although Adrian had also often been away at university.

'I missed my foster carer,' she said, her face clouding over. 'I remember that dreadful feeling that I had been left here for good and no one would ever come back for me.'

I was shocked. I'd done everything I could to make her feel welcome, as I do all the children I foster, and had reassured her it would just be for two weeks, yet here she was, claiming she'd felt as though she'd been left here for good!

CHAPTER TWO

AMBULANCE

It was gone 1 a.m. by the time Lily had washed and finished in the bathroom and was in bed. I'd left the landing light on, as I do with any child who is staying with us so they can see their way to the toilet if necessary. I'd also left the curtains parted in her room as she'd requested, which was apparently what I had done when she was here before. I'd told Lily to call out if she needed anything and had come out of the room. Although there was a lot she wasn't telling me, I thought we'd have a good chat in the morning when everything would become clearer.

Paula had gone to bed, so I knocked on her door and said goodnight.

'How long is Lily staying for?' she asked.

'I'm guessing not long. I'm assuming she'll go back to Maddison's Hostel tomorrow.'

Paula nodded and said goodnight. I came out and closed her bedroom door.

I went to my bedroom and got into bed. I wasn't tired any more. My mind was buzzing as I thought about Lily and what she'd been up to in the last ten years. I didn't have any information. Indeed, I hadn't heard about her at all. I'd just looked after her on respite for two weeks while her foster parents were away. She hadn't mentioned a job, school or college. In fact, she hadn't mentioned anything from her life, just some memories from when she'd stayed with me. Some children arrive and don't stop talking, others hardly say a word. I was intrigued to know why the adoption had broken down. Some parents just don't have the patience when the child reaches puberty. Others try their best, but it doesn't work out. Either way, I sometimes feel that more could have been done earlier to support the placement.

I thought about Lily for some time, and the large ceramic pot in the porch that she'd smashed. Was she really going to spend the night in the porch? I assumed so.

I eventually dropped off to sleep and woke at 7 a.m. The house was quiet, and then I remembered that Lily was with us. If she was awake, I didn't want to leave her lying in bed staring at the curtains. The heating was on – it came on at 6 a.m. – so we rose to a warm house. Paula had that day and the next off work as part of the Christmas holidays. She worked in an administrative position in the offices of a local manufacturing firm and seemed to quite enjoy it.

I got up. I'd leave Paula to have her lie-in. I went round the landing to Lily's room and listened at the door. It was quiet. I opened the door and looked in. I saw Lily was fast asleep so I came out, silently closing the door. I went downstairs and into the kitchen. It was still a mess from yesterday. I'd clean it up later. Sheba rushed to greet me, so I gave her a stroke and her breakfast while the kettle boiled. I also put a slice of toast in the toaster.

Lily's bedroom was directly over the kitchen and the floorboards squeaked. I'd never had them repaired as it allowed me to know when someone was out of bed. I assumed that as soon as someone was up at Maddison's Hostel they would phone me straight away.

I went into the living room and opened the curtains and sat there eating my toast and drinking my coffee. The garden looked very bare in the heart of winter, sorry for itself. I'd swept up the leaves so there was nothing to do out there until spring.

I checked my phone for messages and saw one from Lucy and also Kirsty, thanking me for the nice time they'd had yesterday. Lucy is my other daughter and Kirsty is my daughter-in-law, married to Adrian, my son. Lucy and her partner, Darren, have two children – Emma, seven, and Theo, three. Adrian and Kirsty have one child, Sophia, who is three. They all live quite close to me, which is nice. Adrian is an accountant and Kirsty a teacher. Life is very busy now. I do some respite fostering and also some family support work. I am also asked to give talks from time to time at the carers' introductory evenings. I used to be quite nervous doing this, but now, after many years, I've got used to it. My audience of would-be foster carers are always far more nervous than me and can't wait to chat over coffee when I've finished my lecture.

I sat in the living room daydreaming until 8.30 a.m. when I thought it was time to get dressed. There was still a lot of clearing up to do from yesterday and I like to get it done in the morning. I knew that Paula would help me, but it wasn't her responsibility. Before I left the living room my thoughts went back to yesterday. I had the feeling that Kirsty and Adrian wanted to tell me something and were waiting for the right time. Perhaps it was that Kirsty was expecting their second child. That would be nice. Sophia would be going to school in September. She is a darling, as all my grandchildren are, and I always greatly look forward to seeing them.

I stood and went upstairs. There was no noise coming from either of the bedrooms. I wasn't really expecting to see Paula or Lily for at least another couple of hours. I showered and dressed and returned downstairs to the kitchen, where I began by unpacking the dishwasher from last night and reloading it. By 9.30 a.m. I still hadn't heard from Maddison's. This was plenty late enough for them to have picked up their calls and I needed to know what I was to do with Lily today. I assumed I would put her on the train to return to them. I phoned them again and it went through to voicemail as it had before, so I left another message.

'Hi, it's Cathy Glass. Could someone please phone me? Lily Saunders stayed with me last night.'

I guessed they were short-staffed over Christmas and didn't think much more about it.

Paula appeared in the kitchen at around 10 a.m. looking slightly worse for wear.

'Did Kirsty speak to you yesterday?' she mumbled, pouring water into the kettle.

'No. We didn't get a chance to talk. Why?'

'She and Adrian are thinking of fostering, and she wanted to talk to you about it.'

'Really?' I said, amazed.

'You seem surprised.'

'I assumed they would have another child.'

'Well, that's the thing. I know Kirsty wanted to talk to you about the ins and outs of fostering, so I'll leave it to her.'

'Yes. I see, well, that is unexpected. Aren't they going to try for another child then?' I asked.

'It's highly unlikely that Kirsty will be able to conceive.'

'Oh. She told you that?'

'Yes.'

It was a shock that Kirsty couldn't have any more children. I didn't even know they had been tested, but I knew I needed to wait until Kirsty found the right moment to tell me before bringing it up with her.

By 10.30 a.m. I still hadn't heard from Maddison's. I was starting to get annoyed. I had one of their children with me – didn't they care? So I gave them another half an hour and phoned again. The phone rang and rang and eventually a man picked it up.

'Hello,' was all he said.

'It's Cathy Glass. I left two messages on your voicemail.'

'Yes?'

'Lily Saunders stayed with me last night.'

'Yes?'

'She's one of yours,' I said quietly, seething at his attitude.

'No, she's not,' he said. 'I'll get the deputy manager.'

He put the phone down. What? I thought. He doesn't know what he's talking about – not one of theirs. I waited some more. I could hear voices in the background. Eventually the deputy manager came on the phone.

'I understand you are asking about Lily Saunders?' she said.

'Yes. That's correct. She's here with me.'

'I'm afraid she left Maddison's over a year ago. I don't know where she is now.'

She's with me, I thought again but didn't say.

'I'm sorry, I'm not understanding. Lily told me yesterday she was living at Maddison's.'

'I'm afraid she's not. Sorry. I can't tell you any more,' she said. 'Confidentiality forbids.'

I gave an inward sigh. 'OK. Thank you.'

We hung up.

I sat in the living room. Paula was there looking at me quizzically.

'Lily left Maddison's over a year ago,' I said, perplexed.

'I think you need to wake her and find out what's going on,' she replied.

'Yes. You're right. It's late enough.'

We went straight upstairs and knocked on her bedroom door. There was no reply. I knocked again and went in. She was as I'd left her, lying on her back, eyes closed. Paula waited just inside the door.

'Lily,' I said gently. 'Time to wake up.'

She didn't stir or move a limb.

'Lily,' I said, slightly louder. 'It's time to wake up.'

There was still no response, not even an eyelid flicker, although I noticed she was breathing quite heavily.

'Lily, time to open your eyes,' I tried again, and lightly shook her shoulder.

Her eyes were shut, she didn't stir, but she kept breathing heavily, in and out. Something wasn't right, I thought.

'Lily!' I said more loudly.

Paula came into the room.

'Lily, wake up!' I tried.

I shook her shoulder again, but she still didn't wake. This couldn't be normal sleep. I was starting to feel hot and clammy.

I tried to wake her one more time, then said, 'Paula, can you phone for an ambulance?'

She rushed into her bedroom and came back with her phone, calling 999 as she came. She passed the phone to me.

'Is the patient breathing?' the call handler asked me.

'Yes, but her breathing is heavy. I can't wake her.'

'What's your address?'

I told her.

'An ambulance is on its way.'

'How old is the patient?' she asked.

'Eighteen.'

'Can you try to wake her?' she said.

'I'm shaking her shoulder now but she's not stirring … Lily, come on, wake up,' I said.

'Has she taken any medication?' the call handler asked.

'Not as far as I'm aware. She arrived here last night. I haven't seen her for ten years. I'm a foster carer.'

'An ambulance will be with you shortly.'

At that moment we heard a siren in the distance.

'I can hear it coming,' I said. 'Thank you.'

I handed Paula's phone back to her and asked her to go down to let the paramedics in.

I tried shaking Lily's shoulder again, but there was no response. She was like a large doll, lying flat on her back.

Very soon I heard Paula open the front door and she was asked where the patient was.

'Upstairs,' I heard her say.

There was the sound of footsteps on the stairs, then coming round the landing. Suddenly the room was full as three paramedics came in. I moved away from Lily and went to stand beside Paula just outside the bedroom door, so they could all fit in.

'What's her name?' the first paramedic asked me.

'Lily Saunders,' I said.

'And she's eighteen?'

'Yes.'

The lead paramedic began shaking her shoulder, trying to wake her, much as I had done.

'Wake up, Lily,' he said loudly. Then to me, 'Has she taken anything?'

'I don't know.'

The second paramedic picked up her bag from beside the bed.

'Is this hers?' he asked me.

'Yes.'

He put his hand in and brought out a packet of tablets.

'Did she take these, do you know?'

'I don't know,' I said.

Paula and I continued waiting just outside the bedroom door as the lead paramedic began working on her. He took her blood pressure, her pulse, and then began sticking electrodes on her chest. All the while he was talking to her in a loud voice, telling her to wake up as I had done. But there was no response. One of the paramedics came to the door to talk to us.

'I understand you don't really know her?' he said.

'Not really. She arrived here late last night. My daughter and I were in bed and we got up to open the door. I barely recognized her. I wasn't expecting her. No one had been in touch. I haven't seen her for ten years. She didn't tell us anything about herself other than that she lived at Maddison's, which is a hostel a hundred miles away, but she doesn't. I spoke to them a little while ago and they told me she left there a year ago. That's all they would tell me because of confidentiality. I've no idea where she's been.'

Suddenly Lily made a noise that came from deep within her throat and she was sick.

'Thank goodness,' I said.

'Come on, Lily, wake up now,' the lead paramedic said loudly, turning her onto her side.

Her eyelids eventually began to flicker open.

'Come on, sleepy head, wake up,' he said. 'How many of these have you taken?' He was referring to the packet of tablets he was holding.

'I don't know,' she mumbled. 'About ten.'

I could see that the tablets were from a packet labelled co-codamol.

'We'll take her to the hospital to get her checked over,' the lead paramedic said. 'Do you want to come?'

'Yes, I think I should. She hasn't got anyone else.'

While I got my bag and phone, they brought up an evacuation chair and strapped Lily into it. They bumped her downstairs and she moaned, which I thought was a good sign. I said goodbye to Paula at the front door. She was still in her dressing gown.

'I'll phone,' I told her.

I went outside and got into the ambulance. I sat in the seat opposite Lily, wondering what on earth had led to her trying to take her own life in my house.

CHAPTER THREE

I DON'T TRUST HER

It's about a fifteen-minute drive to the hospital and Lily was half awake during most of it, answering some of the paramedic's questions, groaning at other times and closing her eyes. I wanted to ask why she'd tried to take her life, but it didn't seem appropriate with the paramedics present.

'I wonder why she did it,' I said more than once while her eyes were closed.

'She will be referred to a psychiatrist at the hospital,' the paramedic who was riding with us replied. The two other paramedics were in the front of the ambulance. 'I bet it gave you a shock, going into her room and finding her like that.'

'Yes, it did,' I admitted, and a tear formed in my eye. 'Suppose she had taken more tablets and succeeded in ending her life?' It didn't bear thinking about.

'I think it was probably a cry for help,' he said. 'We get called to many young people who do that. You don't know her medical history, do you?'

'No. She just arrived on my doorstep late last night. I last saw her ten years ago.'

He seemed to find it difficult to believe my account, and I supposed it was incredible. Paula and I had given Lily a bed for the night without knowing anything about her. Would I have done so if I hadn't been a foster carer? I think I might have, and many foster carers would have acted similarly. You see children and young people in a different light through fostering – their vulnerabilities.

We arrived at the hospital and I followed Lily in the chair through to Accident & Emergency. It seemed very busy and there was a drunk man shouting in between two security guards in one corner. Lily was wheeled straight into a cubicle, where she was transferred to the bed in there. She closed her eyes again.

'This is Lily Saunders,' the lead paramedic said to the two nurses. 'She is eighteen years old and of no fixed abode.' Then he gave her vital signs and said she had taken an overdose.

'What's she taken?' one of the nurses asked.

'About ten of these,' he said and passed her the packet of tablets.

The paramedics prepared to leave and so I thanked them before they went.

'Are you her mother?' the nurse asked me.

'No. I'm a foster carer. I haven't seen Lily for about ten years, but she suddenly arrived at my house late last night.'

'Why?'

'I honestly don't know.'

She asked for Lily's full name, which I gave her, but I didn't know her exact date of birth, just the year, which she wrote down.

'Which address shall I put?' she asked.

'Use mine,' I said, and gave it to her.

'Do you know her doctor?' she asked.

'No, sorry. I know nothing about her.'

She began to examine Lily – pulse rate, blood pressure and so forth – then she started to put electrodes on her chest. I could see now how thin Lily was. Her ribs stuck out. The nurse inserted a cannula into her arm, which made Lily moan, but she opened her eyes, which I thought was positive. The nurse took some blood for analysing and left, saying a doctor would be in to see Lily shortly.

Lily dozed but it was a different kind of sleep now. Her breathing was normal. After about a quarter of an hour a young doctor appeared. We went through the same questions I had already answered. I couldn't tell him any more. Then he examined her, listening to her heart and taking her pulse. He checked the ECG reading.

'She's been lucky,' he said. 'She'll recover shortly. I'll make a referral to the psychiatrist, then she'll be able to go home with a referral to her doctor.'

I thanked him as he left our cubicle and breathed a sigh of relief.

'You're going to be all right,' I told Lily.

She turned over in bed.

Gradually, over the next couple of hours Lily woke up properly and asked for a drink. I checked with the nurse if she could have one and she said, 'Yes. It's good to drink.' We'd been there nearly three hours and I'd phoned Paula a couple of times and told her what was happening. There was so much I wanted to know about Lily, but I recognized she needed time to recover.

An hour later the psychiatrist arrived and asked to be left alone with Lily as she was eighteen and an adult. I stood and came out. The psychiatrist was with her for about a quarter of an hour, then reappeared.

'Lily will be referred to the psychiatric team,' was all she said.

'Thank you.'

It was nearly five o'clock when a nurse arrived and said we could go now and removed the cannula from Lily's arm. Lily made a fuss as she watched the needle sliding out. 'Don't look,' I told her, but she did.

Before we left the cubicle I called Paula and asked her to come to collect us from the hospital.

'Is Lily coming back to our house?' Paula asked.

'Yes. As far as I know, she's got nowhere else to go.'

'But supposing she does the same thing again?'

'Then we'll have to rethink. I'll phone around tomorrow and see what I can find out.'

Lily linked her arm through mine for support as we left A&E. We found a seat near the main door while we waited for Paula to arrive. I said to Lily, 'If you're staying with me then I think we need to have a chat, don't you? Maddison's has told me that you left there over a year ago. That's all they've said.'

'Yes,' she said sullenly. 'But I'm very tired right now. Tomorrow would be better.' Which I accepted.

I saw Paula's car pull into the pick-up/drop-off bay at the front of the hospital.

'She's here,' I said, and drew Lily to her feet.

She didn't want to link my arm again as we went out to the car. I opened the rear door and she got in with a sigh. She allowed her head to flop back and closed her eyes.

'Are you OK?' I asked her.

'Yes,' she mumbled.

I got into the passenger seat next to Paula. 'Thanks for picking us up,' I said, and she nodded.

Lily had her eyes closed during the drive home, with her head resting to one side. Every time Paula turned a corner Lily gave a small, exaggerated groan. I kept glancing at her in the interior mirror. I asked her a few times if she was all right and she moaned, 'Yes, I think so.' She'd been far more responsive in hospital, I thought.

Once home, I helped her out of the car and we went into the hall. She said she wanted to go straight to bed as she was very tired. Indeed, it seemed as if she had difficulty standing up now. I wished I'd asked at the hospital what to expect after taking ten co-codamol.

'Do you want something to eat or drink?' I asked her in the hall.

Her eyes opened. 'Egg, bacon and beans would be nice,' she said. 'I know you always have those in the fridge.'

Yet again I was astounded that she could remember this from ten years ago and that she was suddenly wide awake.

'Do you want a drink?' I asked.

'A hot chocolate, please.'

'Do you need help washing and dressing?' I asked.

'No, thank you.'

Nevertheless, I went with her upstairs and saw her into the bathroom. It was now 7 p.m. I left her having a wash and returned downstairs.

'Kirsty phoned the landline while you were out,' Paula told me.

'OK. I'll give her a ring once I've cooked Lily's food.'

I went into the kitchen and began to cook the bacon and eggs while Paula went to her room. I opened a can of beans, microwaved them, put it all on a plate, and made the hot chocolate. I took it all upstairs to Lily. As I neared her bedroom door I heard her talking on the phone, which must have been in her bag. It sounded more like an argument; her voice was raised, and I wondered who she was arguing with. I knocked on her door and went in. The phone must have been quickly put away. It was nowhere to be seen. Lily was sitting on the edge of the bed, looking a lot brighter.

'Is everything all right?' I asked her.

'Yes. Why shouldn't it be?' she asked curtly.

'No reason. I thought I heard you on the phone just now.'

She shrugged, but didn't reply.

'Here's your dinner,' I said, going into the room.

'Can you put it over there?' she asked, referring to the small table, which acted as a desk.

I put the plate on the table with the bottle of tomato ketchup, which I knew most young people liked, and the hot drink.

'Have you got everything you need?' I asked her.

'Yes.'

She looked as though she was waiting to resume the phone call so I came out, drawing the door to behind me. When I was halfway down the stairs, I heard it click too.

Paula, bless her, had cooked our evening meal and she now took the cottage pie from the oven.

'I don't trust her,' she suddenly said to me.

I turned to look at her. 'Who? Lily?'

She nodded.

'That's not like you. You're one of the most trusting people I know.'

'There's something not right about her. All this secrecy. Why can't she tell us what she's been up to?'

'She says she's tired out now and will tell me tomorrow,' I said.

'It's 7.30,' Paula said. 'She's spent all today in bed. How can she be so tired?'

'I guess it's a result of the tablets she took. I'll talk to her tomorrow. She's promised she will.'

'OK, but be careful. Find out what's going on. As far as I can remember we've never had anyone stay who we know so little about. What about phoning her old carer?'

'Yes. I thought of that. I might do if Lily doesn't tell me what's been going on.'

We were in the kitchen and we heard the floorboards squeak. Lily was walking around her bedroom. It continued for some minutes, then stopped. I assumed she'd gone back to bed.

Paula and I ate the cottage pie at the table in the extension. It was delicious and I congratulated her. As soon as we'd finished I went upstairs and knocked on Lily's door.

'Come in,' she called.

I went in and found her in bed. Her plate was empty and on the table. There was no sign of her phone.

'Are you all right?' I asked her.

'Yes, thanks.'

'Is there anything you need?'

'No.'

'Are you in bed for the night?' I asked her.

'Yes. I'll see you in the morning.'

I didn't feel comfortable kissing her goodnight, so I came out.

'Can you close my door?' she called after me.

I pulled it to. Lily seemed far bolder now. In fact, she seemed quite assertive. I went downstairs.

'Don't forget to phone Kirsty,' Paula reminded me.

'I'll do it now.'

It was a conversation I'd hoped I would never have.

CHAPTER FOUR

GONE

'I wanted to tell you personally,' Kirsty began on the phone. 'Adrian isn't good with this type of thing.' Which I knew. He rarely talked about his feelings and often kept them to himself for far longer than he should. 'We didn't tell you about it at the time,' Kirsty continued, 'but when I had Sophia it was discovered I was born with only one ovary. It's a rare condition called unilateral ovarian absence [UOA]. We were very lucky I was able to conceive Sophie, it was a miracle, but I'm afraid there won't be any more babies for us.'

'I'm so sorry,' I said. 'I know you wanted more than one child.'

'Yes, we were very upset when we found out, but we're grateful to have Sophia. We've thought a lot about having more children. We don't want Sophia to grow up alone. We've decided we'd like to foster, like you.' Kirsty paused to take a breath while I said nothing, not yet wanting to voice my feelings. 'We went to the introductory evening last week and we've got a social worker coming to see us in the new year. What can you tell us about fostering? My parents are opposed to it.'

'Why?' I asked.

'They think we are putting ourselves at risk.'

'In what respect?'

'Unfounded allegations. I've told them there are things we can do to protect ourselves.'

'That's right. It's called the "safer caring policy" and it's tailored to the needs of the whole family. It deals with expectations, routines and safeguards, but it won't protect you completely.'

'I've read about it online,' Kirsty said. I could hear the excitement in her voice.

'You know you can't protect yourselves from every eventuality, though,' I emphasized.

'I know. My mother says the social services can take your own children away if an allegation is made against you by the foster child.'

'That's true. Being investigated is not a nice experience. Did you know that 33 per cent of foster carers have experienced an allegation – 14 per cent in the last two years?'

'I read that somewhere,' Kirsty said, undeterred.

'I understand that you want more children, but what does Adrian say about all of this?'

'He's still a little undecided. It is our main worry, what could happen if a child says something against us. We couldn't bear to lose Sophia, not even for a day.'

I inwardly recoiled at the possibility.

'Hopefully it won't ever come to that,' I said realistically. 'But you're right to be prepared.'

I thought of my own children and the danger I'd put them in through fostering for many years. Thankfully, I'd never had an allegation made against me. I think it was more luck than anything, although I was very careful when we had visitors. I know carers who have had an allegation made against them and once it was resolved they stopped fostering completely, and who can blame them? I think more needs to be done to protect carers.

'Why not raise the matter when you see the social worker who is visiting you?' I suggested.

'Yes, we will do. I raised it at the introductory evening, and to be honest it was pushed to one side.'

I hadn't seen Kirsty and Adrian at the introductory evening they had attended, as it was in a different area.

'Oh dear. I am sorry,' I said. 'That isn't the way to deal with it. It's a valid topic for debate. I would raise it again with the social worker, but try not to let it dominate your thinking. There are all the joys that fostering brings to consider.'

'I know, but it is a worry.'

'Have you thought what age group you would like to foster?' I asked, changing the subject. I thought that Kirsty's mother had put too much emphasis on unfounded allegations.

'Five or under,' she said. 'I'm thinking of taking a part-time job in teaching. Will the social services allow that?'

'If the foster child is at school, they will consider it. I would make a list of all the questions you want to ask the social worker.'

'Yes, we are. Can I ask you honestly, would you do it again?' Kirsty said earnestly. I could picture her brow furrowing as she spoke. 'I know it became a way of life for you.'

'Yes, unreservedly, although I might not have done if I'd had an unfounded allegation made against my family.' Which was the truth. I was about to tell her of Lily but decided not to. 'You'll know quite quickly if fostering is for you – by the end of the first year, I would say.'

'That's what Adrian said.'

'What does he say about being part of a family that fostered?' I asked.

'That he'd do it again.'

'That's good.'

I was pleased. It's not often you get direct feedback from your children on fostering. I felt I'd done the right thing. We continued talking for a while about fostering, then we said goodnight. I ended the call deep in thought. Would I recommend a young couple like Kirsty and Adrian to foster? Yes, on balance I think I would.

Paula appeared and I told her what Kirsty had said but she seemed to know already. I wondered if Lucy knew too. News travels fast between my children, sometimes without it touching me.

I went upstairs to check on Lily. She was fast asleep. I returned downstairs and Lucy phoned.

'Hello, love. How are you?' I said.

'Fine. How are you?'

'I'm good, thanks.'

'Kirsty and Adrian are thinking of fostering,' Lucy blurted out, unable to contain the news.

'Yes. Kirsty phoned me just now and we had a long chat.' Which I thought Lucy might already know. 'Kirsty and Adrian have been to the introductory evening for would-be foster carers. They are seeing a social worker soon. They have some concerns about unfounded allegations.'

'Yes, that's what she told me. I wouldn't foster,' Lucy said.

'No? Why not?' I asked.

I was surprised, as Lucy had been in care for the early part of her life and had then come to me, and I adopted her (see my book *Will You Love Me?*).

'It's too much of an upset for the foster family,' Lucy said. 'They don't know if they're coming or going.'

'Did you feel that when you came to me?' I asked, concerned.

'No, you took everything in your stride, but some of the people I stayed with, well, having me there turned their lives upside down and they couldn't cope.'

Interesting, I thought. Lucy had never expressed this view to me before.

'Hopefully, Kirsty and Adrian will take it in their stride. Have they made up their minds yet?' I asked.

'Kirsty says no, but I'm sure they will go ahead with it.'

We talked about fostering for a while, then Theo woke and Darren couldn't settle him so Lucy had to go.

'Speak soon,' she said.

'Yes, love you.'

'Love you too. I wouldn't worry about Kirsty and Adrian; they'll make the right decision.'

That evening I sat and thought about fostering for some time. My life would have been very different without it. I was sure I'd made the right decision to foster for all those years.

Sometime later I said goodnight to Paula, and she went to bed while I put Sheba in her bed, checked on Lily, who was still asleep, then went to bed myself. I was exhausted and soon fell asleep thinking of fostering and Adrian and Kirsty. I wondered what little Sophia would make of it all. She would be spoken to by the social worker who was going to visit them.

I slept well that night and when I woke it was after 7 a.m., but I had a feeling something wasn't right in the house. I threw on my dressing gown and went round to Lily's room. The door was open and when I looked in her room it was empty. I went downstairs to find the front door unlocked. It appeared Lily had gone.

I quickly checked the rest of the house, but there was no sign of her. I went to her room. Her bag and phone had gone too. What should I do? Report her missing to the police or wait?

CHAPTER FIVE

POLICE

Still thinking about Lily – a girl I hardly knew – and where she could have gone, I went into the kitchen to make coffee. I could hear Paula in the bathroom getting ready to go out to meet friends. If I phoned the police and reported Lily missing, what would I say? That an eighteen-year-old who had stayed with me ten years ago for two weeks had arrived on my doorstep late two nights before and had now vanished. What was there to report?

I thought about how, with children who lived permanently in a foster-care situation, you knew their habits and routines and had something concrete to tell the police, plus ideally a photograph to give them. But I had nothing. Yet if something had happened to Lily, I wouldn't forgive myself. I was in a quandary about what to do or not do.

I put down my coffee and went again to Lily's bedroom. I looked around, looked in the wardrobes and drawers. I checked around the mattress, but there was nothing to be seen. She'd arrived with nothing. I'd intended to give her some nearly new clothes from my second-hand box after our chat, but now she'd gone in what she stood up in.

Paula came down to get herself some toast for breakfast.

'Where's Lily?' she asked, having passed her bedroom on the way to the toilet.

'She seems to have gone,' I said.

Paula rolled her eyes and put a slice of toast in the toaster. 'I'm not surprised,' she said.

She didn't say any more and neither did I. I felt sympathy for Lily, and I was sure she had a story to tell me. Paula took her toast upstairs to eat as she got ready to go out, while I continued thinking about whether or not I should report Lily missing to the police. In a way, I felt responsible for her. She'd spent the night here, after all.

Paula came downstairs and, calling goodbye, left the house.

I got dressed still thinking of Lily and at 11 a.m. I phoned our local police station.

'I'm not sure about this,' I began, 'but I think I need to report a person missing.'

I was put through to an officer who asked me what the problem was.

'I am a foster carer. I had a girl, aged eighteen, who arrived without warning the night before last. I hadn't seen or heard from her in ten years. Without saying anything to me or my daughter, who also lives here, she left during last night. I don't know what time and I don't know where she's gone. I know she was in a children's hostel for a time but that was over a year ago.'

The officer was silent for a moment.

'Why do you think she might have come to harm?' he asked.

'I don't know, but she did try to take her own life the other night. Her name is Lily Saunders. Do you think I should file a missing person's report?' I'd done this quite a bit during the years I'd been fostering full time. If Lily had been a child I was looking after, I could have phoned the social services' out-of-hours team for advice before the police.

'I am sure she'll be fine,' he said. 'Wait until the end of the day. If you haven't heard from her then, call us again.'

'Thank you,' I said, and ended the call.

I felt a little relieved.

I stayed in that morning. It was freezing outside, and I had no reason to venture out. It was just as well I didn't go out, for shortly after midday the doorbell rang. When I checked the spyhole I saw Lily standing there, shivering. Grateful, I opened the front door.

'Sorry,' she said, her teeth chattering. 'It's cold out here.'

She was wearing the same thin denim jacket as before and had her small bag over her shoulder.

'Come in,' I said. 'Do you want a hot drink?'

'Yes, a hot chocolate, please, and can I use your toilet?'

'Go ahead.'

She ran upstairs, and I felt pleased she had reappeared. I went through to the kitchen, where I made the hot chocolate. When Lily had finished in the toilet I heard her go quickly into her bedroom, then she came down into the kitchen and stood by the radiator, still shivering.

'You've got very cold,' I said, handing her the hot drink.

'Yes. It's freezing outside.'

'Do you want a jumper?'

'No, I'll be OK.'

I asked her if she wanted something to eat.

'Can I have the same as yesterday, please?'

'Yes, and then we need to talk before you vanish again.' I smiled, but it wasn't returned. 'Why don't you sit at the table and drink your hot chocolate while I cook your breakfast?' This was where the foster children sat while I was in the kitchen.

She went over to the table and sat as I cooked the bacon, egg and beans. Lily spent the time texting on her phone. Once her meal was ready, I took it to the table with a knife and fork. I sat opposite her as she ate ravenously, sipping my cup of coffee. She didn't speak but kept pausing from eating to tap her phone. I waited until she'd finished her meal before I began.

'So, Lily, what's going on?' I asked as non-confrontationally as I could.

'Nothing,' she said with a shrug, and tapped her phone again.

'Could you leave your phone alone and talk to me, please?' I said more firmly.

She looked at me.

'What led you to take all those co-codamol tablets and then clear off during the night?'

'I'm very down,' she said. 'I didn't want to live. I often get like that.'

'I'm sorry to hear that. Are you seeing a doctor or therapist?' I asked.

'I used to, but I stopped going to the therapist. She wasn't doing me any good.'

'Perhaps try another one?' I suggested.

She shrugged.

'Why are you feeling so low?' I asked.

'Don't know. I just am. The smallest things get me down. I'll kill myself one day. I know I will.'

I was shocked but I didn't show it. 'Why did you come to my house the night before last?' I asked.

'My boyfriend lives not far from here and I thought I could stay with him, but I can't. Then I remembered you lived a little way away, so I came here. Sorry about your pot.'

'No worries. I've cleared it up. Did you speak to your boyfriend?' I asked.

'Not really. He's an ex now. That's why I tried to take my life the night before. I went to visit him, but he didn't want to know.'

'Do you have a job, Lily?' I thought this would offer some stability to her otherwise chaotic lifestyle.

'Not at present.'

'What have you been doing since you left Maddison's?'

'I can't remember. It was a long time ago. Sofa-surfing in friends' houses, I think.'

'So you haven't had a permanent home for the last year?'

'No. It's OK, though. I've got used to sleeping on other people's sofas.'

'It's not OK, Lily. You need a proper base. Where did you go last night?'

'To my boyfriend's – ex. I thought about killing myself again, but I'd run out of tablets.'

'Where are all your belongings?' I asked.

'I don't know. I left them wherever I stayed, I guess.'

'So you've got nothing? Just what you are wearing, that bag and your phone?'

'Yes, but I can't pay for it now.'

She looked very down. I knew how much a phone meant to a young person.

'What is it? Pay as you go?'

'No, contract. I got it when I had a job.'

'You worked?'

'For a few weeks.'

'Doing what?' I asked.

'Cleaning, mainly.'

'Have you got any qualifications from school?'

'Some,' she said defensively.

'What do you want to do?'

She looked at me as if I'd just asked if she wanted to go to the moon.

'I don't know.'

'Have the social services not offered you a personal adviser and a plan for your future?'

She looked at me, nonplussed again, and shook her head. I wasn't surprised. She wasn't the only teenager to fall through the cracks. There is provision for someone leaving care at eighteen, but once they'd left their last registered address no one seemed too worried what happened to them.

I looked at her. This was a big decision I was contemplating and I knew I needed to ask Paula first for her view. She didn't seem to think a lot of Lily from what she'd said so far.

'Can I go and have a lie down on my bed now?' Lily asked. 'I've answered a lot of questions, and I didn't sleep well last night.'

'Yes. What time did you leave here?'

'Around 1 a.m.'

'And you went to your ex-boyfriend's?'

'Yes, but they made a fuss and called the police, so I ran away.'

'I don't want you calling your ex again. You will only antagonise his parents.'

'I know,' she said glumly.

She picked up her phone to check it.

'Can I borrow your charger?' she asked. 'My battery is nearly flat. I don't know where mine is.'

'Yes, you can. But we'll plug it in down here. That's where I keep the charger.'

She looked as though she was about to protest but realised that's where I liked my charger kept. I've lost plenty in the past with teenagers borrowing them and then not returning them. She plugged in her phone in the kitchen and then went upstairs for a lie down. A few minutes later the doorbell rang. When I looked through the spyhole I saw what looked like two police officers standing there. Wondering what they wanted, I opened the door.

'Good morning,' the female officer said. 'We understand you have Lily Saunders living here?'

'Not living here. She's staying here today. Can I ask why you want her?'

'She's been making trouble at the home of Mr and Mrs Walters. We understand she dated their son, Steve, for a very short while and won't accept it's over. Her behaviour verges on stalking now.'

'Oh dear. Do you want to come in?'

'Yes, please.'

I opened the door wider to let them in, then showed them through to the living room.

'Lily is upstairs in bed. I think I need to make it clear that she isn't living here. She arrived two nights ago. I hadn't seen her for ten years before that. I looked after her for two weeks on respite. I barely recognized her when she arrived.'

'Can we just have a word with her, please?' the female officer asked.

'I'll fetch her.'

Feeling hot and flustered, I went upstairs and knocked on Lily's bedroom door, then went in. She was lying on her bed with her eyes closed.

'Lily, can you wake up, please? The police are here.'

She groaned and turned over in bed, but I didn't think she was asleep.

'Come on, love. Let's go and see what they have to say. It's about Steve Walters.'

'I know. Do I have to?' she asked, her eyes opening a little as if she was just waking up.

'Yes, you do, or they will come up here to see you. So come downstairs and listen to them. It's the grown-up thing to do.'

'But I'm tired,' she said.

'You can have a sleep once you've seen them. I think you know what it's about' – for she hadn't asked. My first question would have been, 'Why do the police want to see me about Steve?'

'Come on, up you get.'

She groaned again, then slowly hauled herself into an upright position and off the bed. Standing, she put her hand to her head.

'I don't feel so good,' she said, swaying.

'I'm sure you'll be fine once we're downstairs and have got this over and done with.' I'd fostered teenagers before who feigned illness as a means of avoiding what they didn't want to, or couldn't, cope with.

'All right?' I asked her.

She stood holding her head with her hands.

'Let's walk downstairs together,' I suggested.

She slipped her arm through mine and we walked out of her room, downstairs and into the living room. As we entered the room the male officer said, 'Oh dear, it's you.'

CHAPTER SIX

LILY'S PAST

'You know Lily?' I asked him.

'Yes. I recognize her from the last time she was at the police station.'

'Last time?' I asked.

'Yes. For the same charge. Only she left with a caution.'

I could see this was far more complicated than Lily had indicated to me.

'Do you want to sit down?' I asked the officers.

Both officers sat in chairs.

'Lily?' I said.

She was standing in the middle of the room with her head supported by her hands. I still thought her illness was fabricated. She sat on the sofa next to me. I'd had police officers in my house before in connection with children I'd fostered, but to have them here for a child I barely knew was a first for me. The female officer now spoke to Lily.

'You need to leave Steve alone. I know you like him a lot, but the feelings aren't reciprocated. I –'

'What does reciprocated mean?' Lily asked, raising her head and interrupting.

'He doesn't return your feelings,' the female officer said. 'He doesn't want a relationship with you, and as far as I can tell he never has. You need to accept his wishes and leave him alone or you will be arrested the next time and charged. That's three times we have been called to the home of Mr and Mrs Walters late at night. I'm glad you've found somewhere nice to stay.' She glanced around the room.

I was about to protest and say again that she wasn't living here, but I thought better of it.

'OK,' Lily said too easily.

'Do you promise to stay away from Steve's home? You have no reason to go there at all.'

'I can go where I like,' Lily said quite cheekily.

'If we have another call to go there, you will be arrested and charged. Do I make myself clear? You woke up most of the street last night with your noise.'

'Doing what?' I asked, shocked.

'She was shouting and crying hysterically for over an hour. The police were called but you'd fled by the time we arrived. We've just traced you here.'

I looked at Lily. She was unfazed. It seemed to be something of a game for her, running away from the police, and she showed no shame.

'Do you promise you will stay away from Steve's house?' the female officer asked again.

'I guess so,' Lily said. 'There is no reason for me to go there any more if he doesn't want to see me.'

'Exactly,' the female officer said. 'No reason at all.'

'I said OK,' Lily blurted.

'Right. We've said enough, but try to make the most of the opportunity you have here. Turn your life around. I know you had a rough start, but that needn't guide your whole life. You're young. You've got potential. Use it.' I could see the officer was annoyed.

They stood and said goodbye to Lily, who was now sulking, then I saw them to the front door.

'Good luck,' the female officer said to me. 'You'll need it.'

I smiled grimly. 'Thank you.'

I closed the front door and returned to the living room and looked at Lily.

'You must never go to Steve's house again,' I said. 'Or you'll be charged with stalking. Do you understand?'

'I guess so.'

'How do you know him anyway?' I asked.

'He's a friend of a friend. I contacted him two months ago.'

'So you contacted him out of the blue?'

'That's right. That's how you make friends, isn't it?'

Good grief, I thought, no, it isn't.

'Lily, can I ask you, have you ever had a close, meaningful relationship with Steve?'

She looked at me oddly. 'No, I just turned up at his place and we had sex. His parents were out. He thought all his Christmases had come at once.'

I bet he did, and I started to think that perhaps Lily had mental-health issues.

Lily now said she needed to lie down, so I let her go upstairs.

'Can I take your charger with me?' she asked, heading for the kitchen.

'No. Leave it there, please.'

I heard her huff as she went into the kitchen, where

she pulled her phone from the charger, which I then heard drop to the floor. Then she stormed upstairs and shut her bedroom door with far more force than was necessary. I thought she was used to getting her own way.

What was I to do with her? I had a girl in my home who, from the little I knew about her, made me uncertain and worried around her. Was she dangerous? I sat and thought about it, then I decided to phone her last foster carer. Yes, it was a long time ago, but it would be a start. Perhaps she could point me in the right direction to find out more about Lily.

I went to my locked drawer in the front room where I kept my fostering paperwork and rummaged through the files until I found Lily Saunders. There wasn't a lot; she'd only been with me for two weeks, after all. I read the brief paperwork but couldn't find anything untoward there. It was mainly her likes and dislikes, particularly regarding food, of which there'd been many. The carer was Susan Burn. I remembered her, but it occurred to me that she might not even have the same telephone number as she did all those years ago.

I poured a glass of water first and went into the living room, where I closed the door. Sheba had come in and was curled up by the radiator. I sat on the sofa and keyed in Susan's number, my heart starting to thump loudly. Her phone was answered straight away.

'Hello, it's Cathy Glass. I don't know if you remember me. I used to be a full-time foster carer.'

'Yes, of course,' she said delighted. 'How are you?'

'Good, thanks. How are you?'

'Yes. We're doing all right. We're still fostering.'

'That's great.'

You make a lot of friends when you foster and you keep in touch with a few.

'You looked after Lily Saunders for us for two weeks,' she said. 'That must be ten years ago now.'

'Yes. It was.' Foster carers never forget the children they look after. 'It's about Lily that I want to talk to you, actually.'

'Really?' she said, astonished. 'But we haven't seen her for over nine years. We went to the post-adoption meetings, then didn't hear any more from them. I understand the adoption didn't work out.'

'That's right. Lily arrived on my doorstep the night before last.'

'Oh. I didn't know you had kept in touch with her.'

'I haven't. Apparently, she contacted a lad who lives locally, then she came down here on the off-chance and went to his home. He didn't want to see her, so she made a fuss. The police have been called on a number of occasions, and she came here to me late on Boxing Day night.'

'What!' she exclaimed. 'Oh dear.'

'I was wondering what you knew of Lily. I'm very concerned. I'm not sure what to do with her.'

'No, quite. We looked after her for two years until they found a couple who wanted to adopt her. She wasn't the easiest child to place. She was very angry sometimes, but could also be very sweet. She'd had a rough start in life, but I thought we'd found the right couple. I am so sorry you've had this to deal with. What will you do with her?'

'I'm not sure. What do you know of Maddison's? It's a hostel for teenagers up North. Lily was there for some time until a year ago.'

'Sorry, I don't know anything about them. I've never heard of it. As I say, we lost contact with her nine years ago.'

'Do you know which year she left the adoptive parents?'

'No, but I can find their details. Would you like them?'

'Yes, please.'

She paused. 'I think I'd better phone them first and then pass on your number, if that's all right. I'll ask them to phone you.'

'Yes, of course. Tell them I'm trying to build a picture of Lily and what's she's been doing during the last ten years.'

'Then what will you do? She must be eighteen now and out of care.'

'Yes, she is. I'm not sure what to do at present. I can't just throw her out on the streets.'

'No. Let me give the adoptive parents a ring now. It was Jasmine and Luke, I think.'

'Thank you so much.'

'Then let's get together for a coffee one time.'

'Yes, that would be nice. Once I've decided what to do with Lily.'

'Of course. I'll phone you.'

I ended the call and went up to check on Lily. She was fast asleep, and I thought she needed to get into a better routine with her sleeping. I returned downstairs – it was now 3.30 p.m. and I hadn't done anything. I took a large Quorn pie out of the freezer and prepared vegetables for dinner. Half an hour later the phone rang; it was Jasmine Taylor, Lily's adoptive mother.

'Thank you for contacting me,' I said. 'Did Susan tell you why I wanted to speak to you?'

'Yes, sort of. I must admit I got quite a shock when she said who she was. I understand that Lily is with you now?'

'Yes, she's been here for two nights.'

'So she left Maddison's?'

'A year ago.'

'I see. She wouldn't have anything to do with us. We tried calling her at Maddison's, but she refused to speak to us and Maddison's wouldn't tell us anything.'

'When did she go to Maddison's?' I asked.

'When she was fourteen, nearly fifteen.'

'So she was with you for some years?'

'Yes. We did all we could for her, but in the end she said she wanted her freedom more than she wanted us. It caused a lot of upset. After she left we heard she was pregnant, but I think she had a termination. She must have been sixteen then.'

'Oh dear. I am so sorry.'

'Why has she come to you?' Jasmine asked. She was a softly spoken woman who seemed calm and measured in her response. I couldn't imagine her being confrontational or antagonistic.

'I live close to the lad she came down here to see,' I replied.

'I didn't know she knew anyone from where you live.'

'She didn't. She met him two months ago, through a friend of a friend, but he doesn't want anything more to do with her, so she came to me.'

'That sounds like Lily. Where is she now?'

'Upstairs, asleep in bed.'

'Oh dear. She can come back to us, but I don't think she wants to. We have a younger boy living with us,

Jason. He's ten now. He's lovely, but he has learning difficulties so requires a lot of attention. Lily always said we loved him more than we loved her, which is utter nonsense. We loved them both equally.'

'I think many foster children feel that way. But you'd have her back to live with you if she wanted to come?' I asked.

'Yes. It broke our hearts when she kept running away. We had a few reasonably stable years with her, then she started to kick off and refused to come home or go to school. As far as I know she hasn't got any qualifications. We had to move on in the end. We couldn't keep running after her. She took over our lives. She said she wanted to live with others her age, so the social services found her Maddison's.'

'I see. I think it would be better if she could come back to you. She knows you. She doesn't seem to have any direction in her life. She's got no job and just seems to float around and has been for the last year. Do you want to discuss it with your husband?'

I knew that carers often made rash offers to look after a child and then bitterly regretted it later. It seemed as if Jasmine and Luke had done all they could for Lily at the time, but at least they knew her and what she was capable off.

'Yes. I'll talk to him this evening when he gets home from work. I'll call you back. I doubt she'd come back to us, though. I'd love to see her again. Will you tell her that?'

'Yes, of course. Thank you for your time. You've been a big help.'

'You're welcome.'

As Jasmine finished speaking, I thought I heard a tear catch in her throat. She seemed lovely, a very nice lady who had done her best to keep Lily.

CHAPTER SEVEN

THE PHONE

I continued sitting in the living room thinking of Jasmine. She wasn't the person I was expecting, not at all. Some carers can be harsh in their condemnation of ex-foster children, but she and Luke had done their best for Lily for many years. If Jasmine said that she and her husband were willing to offer Lily a home, then I would need to be very diplomatic when I put the offer to Lily. I'd formed the impression that she was a young person who was at the mercy of her feelings and could react badly. Would she go back and get a job or go to college and settle into a routine? It troubled me that at such a young age she'd already been pregnant.

After a while I went upstairs to look in on Lily. She was lying on her bed texting on her phone.

'Hi, love,' I said.

'Just a minute,' she said to me.

I waited until she'd finished sending the message. She looked at me and I sat beside her on the bed.

'I think you should know that I've spoken to Susan Burn and Jasmine Taylor.'

She stared at me and her face clouded over.

'What did you want to call them for?' she asked quite rudely.

'To get a better picture of you. You haven't really told me anything about who you are.'

'It's none of your business. I'm an adult. I can do what I want.' She returned to her phone.

Had I told her not to be so rude, I knew she would have simply left.

'Can we have a chat, please, Lily?'

'If you want.'

'Can you put your phone down?'

She put the phone face down on the bed in a huff.

'Jasmine has told me that she and Luke still think a lot of you.'

'No, they don't, and I'm not going back there.'

'I think you're still suffering.'

'She prefers Jason to me.'

'No, she doesn't. They love you both equally. Have you got anywhere else to go?'

But she'd picked up her phone again and begun texting.

'OK, love, we'll talk again. I'm going downstairs to make us dinner. You know where I am if you need me.'

She ignored me and continued texting. I hoped she wasn't texting Steve.

I fed Sheba, who was meowing around my legs, and then got on with making dinner.

I listened out for Lily, but there was no sound from her. I popped into her room at one point and she was still texting. She asked me quite rudely what I wanted.

'Just checking you're all right,' I said.

She grunted, but I couldn't ignore the fact that she'd already taken an overdose. I returned downstairs and to the kitchen. It was something of a relief when Paula returned. I felt normality had resumed.

'Hi,' she called from the hall.

'Hi, love, I'm in the kitchen.'

She took off her shoes and came through, where she presented me with a lovely bouquet of flowers.

'What have I done to deserve this?' I asked, smiling.

'I didn't think I was very nice about Lily. I'm sorry. I know you can't just tell her to leave.'

'Oh, love, you shouldn't have done this. They're beautiful.' I kissed her cheek.

'You're welcome. I'll get changed. Is Lily still here?'

'Yes. I've spoken to her foster carer today, the one who looked after her when she lived down here, and also to her adoptive mother, Jasmine. She suggested that Lily goes back to live with her. She's asking her husband this evening. Lily says she doesn't want to go.'

'Why not?'

'I don't know. Jasmine seems a lovely person.'

'Perhaps Lily will want to go when she's had time to think about it.'

'Yes,' I agreed. 'I'll put these in water, thanks again.' I gave her another kiss.

While Paula went upstairs to change her clothes, I arranged the flowers in a vase. They looked really beautiful, a mixture of irises, roses and camellias. I placed them on the coffee table in the living room, thinking how sweet it was of Paula.

When dinner was ready, I went upstairs and told Paula, then continued to Lily's room. Her door was closed so I knocked.

'Yes?' came her voice, down and sultry.

I opened her bedroom door and put my head round.

'Dinner is ready,' I said.

'I'm not hungry,' she said, looking at her phone.

'I'd like you to come down and eat what you want. You haven't had anything today.' I stood by the door and waited. 'Come on,' I encouraged.

'My phone needs charging anyway,' she said in a huff, and pulled herself off the bed.

We went downstairs to the kitchen, where Lily plugged her phone into the charger and then sat at the table. Paula joined us.

'Hi,' she said to Lily.

'Have you got a phone charger I can use?' Lily asked Paula.

'My phone is plugged in it at present,' she said.

Lily sighed.

'Your phone will have some charge in it by the time we've finished eating,' I told Lily.

I'd need to get Lily a phone charger if she was staying for a few days, I thought, but I had the feeling it would get lost quite quickly like all her other belongings. I plated up dinner, the pie with carrots, peas and potatoes. It was a real winter warmer.

'Thanks, Mum,' Paula said as I handed her the plate. 'This looks delicious. I'm starving.'

She picked up her knife and fork and immediately began eating. I did likewise. Lily sat and with her head in her hands, staring at her food. She was very thin and hadn't eaten all day. It crossed my mind that she might have the beginnings of an eating disorder, as Lucy had when she'd first come to live with me. Eventually she picked up her cutlery and cut a small piece of pie and put it into her mouth. She chewed it slowly, then swallowed. I didn't know whether she liked it or not. She ate half her meal, which was something. Paula had finished.

'Dessert?' I asked them both.

'Later, please,' Paula said.

'What is it?' Lily asked.

'There's yoghurt, fruit, and I can warm up a pudding.'

'I'll think about it,' Lily said, and I saw Paula roll her eyes.

If I'm honest, there'd been an atmosphere during the whole of dinner. Lily hadn't spoken a word, and I thought that Paula had been guarded in what she said, which wasn't much. Lily got up from the table and took her phone from the charger and went upstairs. I saw Paula start to relax. May as well get it over and done with, I thought.

'Paula, I need to ask you about something. Can Lily stay tonight and possibly for a few days while I sort out where she's going to live permanently?'

'Yes. I thought she would be,' she replied.

I smiled. 'Thank you, love. I appreciate your understanding.' This was her house too, after all.

Paula helped me load the dishwasher, then went upstairs to relax. I'd just plugged my phone back into the charger when it rang. It was Jasmine.

'I've spoken to my husband, Luke, and to Jason, and they agree that if Lily wants to come and live with us then she should. This is her home. She knows this area and still has some friends here.'

'That's great,' I said. 'I'm so pleased.'

'But we would like to visit her first. Can we come tomorrow?'

'Yes, sure.'

'Jason wants to be certain she isn't going to be as horrible to him as she used to be. If she wants to, she can return with us tomorrow.'

'I understand. What time will you arrive?'

'It will be around lunchtime. Say twelve-ish?'

'Yes. Do you want something to eat?'

'No, I'm going to bring sandwiches and drinks with us.'

'OK, fine. We'll see you tomorrow then.'

I decided I'd tell Lily they were coming rather than just have them arrive, so I went upstairs to her room. The door was closed. I gave a perfunctory knock and opened it. As I went in she put her hand over her phone. She'd been speaking on it, and again I hoped it wasn't to Steve.

'Yes? What do you want?' she asked.

'Jasmine and family are coming to see us tomorrow.'

'OK,' she said, desperate to get back to her phone.

'When you've finished I'd like a chat with you,' I said.

'I've got to go,' she told the person on the phone and bluntly ended the call.

'Can I come in?' I asked.

'If you want.'

I went in and sat on the edge of the bed.

'What's the matter?' I asked. 'I get the feeling that something big is bothering you.'

'I haven't got any money for my phone,' she said.

I nearly smiled. 'I can give you some money, but I don't think that's the reason for your hostility, is it?'

She looked down at her phone.

'My life is shit,' she said.

'In what respect? What would you like to change?'

'Everything. I haven't got any credit for my phone, for one thing.'

'But I thought it was on contract?' I said.

'No, they changed it when I couldn't pay. I have to buy it from a shop now and I haven't got any money.' She pulled a face.

'I can give you some money to pay for your phone,' I said.

'Will you?' she said, brightening a little.

I thought she was a difficult young person to assess, although I'd only known her a few days.

'Can we go now?' she asked, jumping off the bed.

'In a minute. I want you to tell me what else is bothering you. Can I ask you, do you do drugs?' I'd seen her type of behaviour in other young people who took drugs. They could be very volatile, inconsistent and not open to reason.

'No. I can't afford to buy drugs, although I tried a friend's once about three years ago. It was horrible.'

Suddenly her phone rang and without thinking she answered it. I thought I heard a woman's voice, very loud and angry. Then it was as though Lily remembered I was there, for she quickly cut the call without speaking.

'Who was that?' I asked. 'She sounded very upset.'

'No one,' she replied, and flushed up.

'Is there anything you want to tell me?' I asked.

She shook her head. 'Can I buy my phone credit now?'

'Yes. I'll come with you. I could do with a walk.'

'I can go alone,' she said.

'I'd like to come. I haven't been out all day,' I insisted. 'When we get back I'll get you some clothes from my store and you can have a shower.' She was looking quite ruffled now and hadn't had a shower since she'd arrived.

I went into Paula's room and told her I was popping to the local shop to buy some phone credit for Lily's phone, and I asked her if she wanted anything.

'A Tony's chocolate bar,' she said, her eyes lightening.

'OK. Anything else?'

'No, thanks.'

I then found a coat in my store that I thought would fit Lily, and she put it on.

'It doesn't look very nice,' she said.

'It will keep you warm.'

I checked to see where Sheba was and found her in her usual spot by the radiator in the living room. We went out into the street. It was pitch dark. I breathed in the fresh, cold night air. I love walking in the evening in winter. I find it therapeutic, although I haven't had to do it for a while. Lily walked beside me, moaning about how cold it was. She had her hands tucked deep inside her coat pockets.

'I bet you're glad you're wearing that coat,' I said.

She shrugged but didn't reply.

As we got to the top of the street she looked to her right.

'Steve lives down there,' she said. 'In Manson Street.'

I knew where that was, about five roads away.

'I hope you weren't thinking of contacting him again, were you?'

She didn't reply.

'Lily, if you contact him again, I'm sure his parents will report you to the police.'

She shrugged and I knew then that she had been in contact with him.

'Please don't,' I said. 'I don't want to see the police again.'

She didn't reply. We crossed the road and went into the corner shop where I said hello to Mr Lee, the owner; his name was printed on a board above his shop. He was used to me coming in here with the children I fostered. He said hi to Lily too, but she didn't reply. I bought her phone credit and Paula's chocolate bar, then I asked Lily if she'd like a chocolate bar. She quickly picked up a handful of bars, which I paid for. She ate two going home!

Once indoors, I found her some spare clothes in my 'nearly new' box. There weren't many items in her size. Lily didn't seem very interested in clothes as many of her age are. I also found her a nightdress. I thought there was less chance of her running away wearing a night dress. I gave her the clothes and took those she'd been wearing to wash, then I left her to shower. She was in and out in two minutes and I assumed she brushed her teeth using the toothbrush I'd left out for her.

Once she was settled in bed, I went in to say goodnight. She'd eaten another two chocolate bars and was on her phone to goodness knows who, chatting and laughing.

'Goodnight, love,' I said.

She gave a small wave.

She seemed happier now, but how long would that last? I wondered. I was looking forward to seeing Jasmine and Luke tomorrow.

CHAPTER EIGHT

JASMINE, LUKE AND JASON

I didn't sleep well again that night. I was half listening out for Lily and went to her room to check on her a couple of times. She was fast asleep. When I woke in the morning I immediately went to her room again but found her still asleep. Paula was asleep too – it was 6.30 a.m. and the Christmas break, so it wasn't surprising. I went downstairs, fed Sheba, then made myself a coffee, which I took upstairs to the bathroom. I like to be up and dressed before any child we have staying with us.

Downstairs again, I took Lily's clothes out of the dryer, folded them and put them to one side. I heard Paula get up at 8.30 but nothing from Lily's room. Paula came down at 9 a.m. for a tea. At 9.45 I stuck my head around Lily's bedroom door. She was still fast asleep and breathing normally. I guessed she was very tired, but at 10.30 I thought she should get up. We had Jasmine and family arriving at 12. I picked up Lily's clothes and went up to her room, where I knocked loudly on her door.

'Are you awake now?' I asked, going in.

She was. 'I was sick in the night,' she said groggily, pointing to the waste-paper basket.

I now saw a tiny bit of vomit or saliva in the bin.

'Oh dear. Did you eat all those chocolate bars last night?' I said, looking around the room. There must have been six in all.

'Yes, but it wasn't those.'

'I can't think it was anything else,' I said.

'It was your chicken pie.'

'It was actually Quorn, and Paula and I ate it and we're fine. You should have called me during the night when you were sick. Shall I fetch you a glass of water or a cup of tea? We've got Jasmine and family arriving later,' I reminded her.

'I'll get up and come down,' she said despondently.

'See how you feel once you're up.'

I checked she had the clothes she needed for the day and put the others in a drawer.

'You don't feel sick any more, do you?' I asked, picking up the waste-paper basket.

'No, it's gone now.'

'Good girl. Come down once you're dressed.'

I went out of her room, closing the door behind me, and then downstairs. I emptied the waste-paper basket into the kitchen bin and gave it a good clean. Thank goodness she'd had the sense to use it, I thought. I'd had children throw up all over the carpet before, and it took a long while before the smell had completely gone.

Half an hour later Lily appeared downstairs, looking a little pale.

'How are you?' I asked.

'OK, I guess.' She shrugged.

'Do you fancy some breakfast?'

'Just some juice. What time is Jasmine coming?' she asked. I could tell she was nervous. She kept chewing her little finger.

'Around twelve, but don't worry, you'll be fine. They just want to see you.'

'It wasn't good when I left before.'

'But that was quite a few years ago. They've forgiven you now. It was Jasmine who suggested they come.'

I poured her the juice and handed it to her.

'Nothing to eat?' I checked.

'No.'

Which I accepted. Six chocolate bars would have unsettled her stomach. I usually have a piece of one.

'Where's Paula?' Lily asked.

'In her room.'

'I'll go and see her.'

'OK, but knock first and wait until she calls "come in".'

'It's like Maddison's Hostel,' she said, and went upstairs.

I heard her knock on Paula's bedroom door, then Paula call, 'Who is it?'

'It's Lily,' she said, going in.

Paula would tell her when she'd had enough, and I guessed Lily would rather see her than meet Jasmine, Luke and Jason. I assumed they were the reason she had gone in there.

I checked that the living room was tidy, which it was – there wasn't really anyone living here to make a mess – and at 11.40 the doorbell rang. I assumed it was Jasmine arriving early. I went down the hall and opened the door. Not Jasmine and family, but a single male.

'Are you Mrs Glass?' he asked nervously.

'Yes.' I'd never seen the man before.

'I'd like to talk to you about Lily Saunders. I understand she's living here.'

'Sort of,' I said. 'What's it about?'

'She's claiming my son made her pregnant.'

I felt the ground shift beneath my feet.

'And you are?' I asked.

'Dave Walters, Steve's father.'

'I think you'd better come in,' I said.

I led the way down the hall and into the living room, where I closed the door. The Christmas decorations moved in the breeze.

'Sit down,' I said. 'Lily is upstairs with my daughter.'

He sat on the edge of the armchair, barely able to contain himself.

'Lily phoned yesterday and told Steve she was pregnant and it was his. I'm not so sure she is pregnant. Do you know? She's been causing us a lot of bother recently. We called the police. She seems loopy to me. Doolally.'

I took a deep breath and tried to get my thoughts together.

'I've only known Lily for a few days,' I began. 'I'm a foster carer and ten years ago I looked after her for two weeks. That was the last I'd heard of her. We found her on the doorstep late on Boxing Day night. She hasn't said anything to me about being pregnant. According to Lily, she had sex once with Steve two months ago.'

'That's what he told us, which is why I'm not so sure she is pregnant. My wife is so upset and angry she couldn't come here today to see you. She phoned Lily yesterday, but Lily just hung up on her.'

'I'm sorry,' I said. 'This is all news to me too. I think you need to leave it with me so I can talk to Lily and find out what is happening and what she wants to do.'

'If she is pregnant, we'll organize a termination,' he said very quickly. 'My son has acted foolishly and regrets it. He has his whole life ahead of him. He is at university. He will be ruined because of one silly night. I'm so angry with him.'

He looked like a man who was struggling to contain his anger.

'Let me talk to her,' I said. 'It's a shock for me too. Do you know where Lily has been living for the last two months?' It had crossed my mind that perhaps it was with Steve and his family.

'No. I assumed here with you.'

I shook my head.

'You seem like a nice person,' he said.

The implication being that Lily wasn't. I thought he'd offered to pay for a termination a bit too quickly for my liking too. If Lily was pregnant then she'd presumably need time to think about her options. It had to be Lily's decision.

'Can we swap mobile numbers?' he said, taking out his phone.

We exchanged numbers, entering them on our phones.

'I'll be in touch when I've spoken to Lily,' I said.

I saw him out. I felt hot and sweaty. I stayed in the hall, thinking how to approach Lily. She was very volatile and hadn't said anything to me about being pregnant. I thought I needed to have a talk with her so I went upstairs. Paula's bedroom door was open a little. I knocked and went in. The atmosphere seemed very sombre.

'I've just had Dave Walters here,' I said to Lily.

'I know. I heard his voice. I expect he told you I was pregnant.'

'Yes. He did.'

I glanced at Paula, who didn't seem shocked by the news.

'Paula says it's my decision whether I have the baby or not,' she said as though she had got one over on me.

'I think we need to talk about this more after Jasmine has been.' This put a different light on her visit. 'Are you going to tell Jasmine?' I asked.

'Yes. It's my baby and I want to keep it this time,' she said defensively.

'Have you seen a doctor or done a pregnancy test?' I asked.

Lily looked at me, dumbfounded. 'No. Why?' she asked.

'It will confirm that you are pregnant.'

'But I know I am. I've missed a period, or I'm late at least.'

'I still think you need to do a test. There could be other reasons why your period is delayed.'

'Like what?' she asked quite aggressively.

'Worry, for one thing.'

'I'm not worried about anything,' she snapped.

At that moment the doorbell rang and I looked at my watch. It was 12.10.

'Is that Jasmine?' Lily asked, suddenly looking anxious.

'I would think so. Let's go downstairs.'

'I'm not coming,' Lily said bluntly, and went out of Paula's room and into her bedroom.

'I'll stay up here, Mum,' Paula said to me.

I went downstairs, now feeling perturbed and agitated. I took a breath before opening the front door. A family of three stood there.

'Cathy?' the woman asked.

'Yes, Jasmine?' I tried to smile.

'This is Luke and Jason,' she said.

'Hi, come in.'

I took them through to the living room. Jasmine looked around as if she expected to see Lily there.

'Lily is upstairs for now. Would you like a drink?' I asked them.

Jason said a very polite, 'No, thank you.'

'I'm fine. I packed a coffee,' Jasmine said. I could tell she was nervous.

'I will ask Lily to come down, although she's said she won't at present.'

'Oh. Would it help if I went up to her?' Jasmine asked. She knew her better than I did.

'Let me check,' I said.

I went upstairs to Lily's room. She'd left her bedroom door open and was sitting on the bed.

'Lily,' I said. 'Jasmine wondered if she could come up here to see you.'

'What for?' she asked rudely.

'To talk to you, that's all.'

'About what?'

'General stuff. She seems very nice.'

'Have you told her I'm pregnant?'

'No, because we aren't certain you are yet.'

'I'll tell her,' she said, and marched off out of her bedroom and downstairs.

It was almost as if she felt satisfied that she had something to be provocative about – to tell Jasmine she was pregnant.

'Mum,' Paula said as I passed her bedroom door, 'do you want me down there too?'

'Only if you want to come.'

'I'll stay up here for now.'

Paula didn't like confrontation any more than I did.

I continued downstairs and into the living room. Everyone was sitting there stony-faced.

'I've just told them I'm pregnant,' Lily said from the centre of the room. She looked as though she was conducting an orchestra.

'Sit down, Lily,' I said. 'I think Jasmine needs an explanation.'

'You didn't say anything on the phone,' Jasmine said, looking at me.

'No, I've only just found out,' I said. 'Dave Walters, the lad's father, called round just before you arrived and told us. But Lily hasn't done a pregnancy test yet.'

'But I'm pregnant like I was before,' she blurted out vehemently. 'And I'm not giving it up this time.'

'Will you sit down, please?' I said more firmly.

She flounced to the sofa and sat. Jasmine was looking at her intently. Luke was concentrating on Jason. I wasn't sure he needed to be hearing all of this.

'That puts a slightly different angle on things,' Jasmine said.

There was an awkward silence.

'Are you sure you don't want a drink?' I asked.

'I'll have one, please,' Jason said.

'And me,' Luke said.

'Jasmine?'

'No, thank you. I'm fine.'

I went into the kitchen. Luke and Jason followed me out, perhaps sensing that Jasmine needed to talk to Lily alone.

'There are some toys in that cupboard,' I said to Jason. I pointed to the cupboards in the extension. 'Help yourself.' Then I said to Luke as I filled the kettle, 'I'm sorry to put all this on you. Half an hour ago I had no idea.'

'Lily can make things up,' Luke said dispassionately.

'Yes. I'll buy a pregnancy testing kit later. She says she wants to keep it.'

'I'm not sure if we can offer her a home in that case. It depends where she wants to live. If she wants to come back to our area then we could possibly look after her for a few months.'

'Let's wait and see,' I said.

I asked Jason what he wanted to drink and he said milk. I poured him a glass and offered him the biscuit tin. He took out a chocolate biscuit.

'Bring those cars with us,' I told him, gesturing to the toys Jason had picked, as I carried the tray of cups into the living room.

Jasmine was trying to talk to Lily, but it sounded as if Lily kept bringing the conversation back to her pregnancy. She spoke loudly when she was excited, only half finishing a sentence. As I put the tray down she flounced out and went upstairs to her room. She hadn't even acknowledged Jason, not once.

CHAPTER NINE

UNHELPFUL

I think we all breathed a sigh of relief as Lily left the room. I glanced at Jasmine and Luke and then at Jason, who was sitting on the floor playing with the toy cars.

'You know Lily a lot better than I do,' I said to Jasmine. 'Is this normal behaviour for her?'

'Yes, sadly, it is. She acts a lot younger than she is,' Jasmine said. 'She can be very volatile and difficult to please.' She shook her head in despair.

'What education did she have?' I asked, and picked up my cup. 'Maddison's wouldn't tell me anything.'

'They were unhelpful with us too,' Jasmine said. 'They wouldn't tell us anything after she'd gone to them. As far as I know her education fell away when she left us. She didn't get any GCSEs. I don't think she even sat them. I've no idea what she's been doing for the last year.'

'Sofa-surfing from what she's told me,' I said, and took a sip of my tea.

'Is Lily going to live with us again?' Jason suddenly asked, looking up. He was pushing a bright-yellow dumper truck along the floor and making *brum-brum* noises.

'We're not sure at present,' Luke said to him.

'I think it would only be for a short while if she did come back,' Jasmine said. 'She hasn't exactly thrown her arms around us and hugged us. I'm not sure if she is pleased to see us or not.'

'I wondered if she was taking drugs, but Lily says no,' I offered.

'I don't think she does,' Jasmine replied. 'She had a very abusive early childhood and I think that's left its mark.'

I nodded in agreement. There was silence again, interspersed by the occasional *brum-brum* noise. I smiled at Jason.

'I had expected to offer her a home,' Jasmine continued. 'Do you think we should?' she said to Luke. 'It's a big commitment. I thought she might have changed.'

'I guess we could for a short while. But do you want her to stay with you?' he asked me.

This meeting wasn't going the way I'd envisaged. They'd obviously had second thoughts now that they'd seen Lily and were back-tracking.

'I honestly don't know,' I said. 'She seems very disorganised. If you definitely aren't going to offer her a home then of course she can stay here for a while. I wouldn't just tell her to go. But there is the pregnancy test to sort out.'

'I don't think she's pregnant,' Luke said bluntly. 'I remember we had all this before. Every month she was late and pregnant.'

'Then she was,' Jasmine said thoughtfully. 'Shall I go upstairs and speak to her?' I'll ask her if she wants to come back with us. I'm assuming nothing is going to happen with the lad who made her pregnant?'

'If she is pregnant,' Luke put in again.

'His father offered to pay for a termination this morning,' I said.

'I'll go up and have a talk with her. As far as I can see, there is nothing to keep her down here. Jason, is that OK with you?'

He nodded.

'Good boy.'

Jasmine stood and went upstairs while I sat there, full of misgivings. Was it best for Lily to go back with them? I wasn't sure now. If she went, I could see her reappearing on my doorstep in no time at all. Paula was still in her room and had closed the door. Five minutes passed, then we heard Lily explode.

'No! I'm not coming with you. Never! I'm staying here near Steve. He'll love the baby and look after us both. I know he will.'

Lily sounded very angry, but I didn't want to go up and intrude. Jasmine knew her a lot better than I did. I went to the bottom of the stairs and called up, 'Is everything all right?'

Lily stormed onto the landing and shouted, 'I'm not going with her. I'm staying here.'

'I've heard you,' I said. 'Come down now, please.' I thought she could do herself damage, she was so wild.

Instead of coming down, Lily ran into her bedroom and slammed the door shut, while Jasmine appeared on the landing and then made her way slowly downstairs.

'I tried,' she said, looking at me.

We went into the living room again.

'Well, I guess that's it,' Luke said. 'We did our best. You know where we are if you need any advice.'

'Yes. Thank you,' I replied.

They stayed for about another ten minutes. Lily was upstairs, ostensibly in her room, but I thought I heard her door open, so I guessed she was listening on the landing. We didn't say anything else about her, but we all knew the decision had been made. Lily wasn't going to live with the Taylor family, now or ever again.

When it was time for them to leave Jason was still playing on the floor with the large yellow dumper truck. The back lifted up. I told him he could take it with him.

'Are you sure?' Jasmine asked.

'Yes.' I felt sorry for the child. He was obviously special needs and just went along with the flow. 'Will you foster again?' I asked as we stood.

'No. We have Jason,' Luke replied. 'And I've got children from a previous relationship.'

I'm sure they were good parents who had just taken on too much with Lily. Some carers only ever foster one child long term. We went into the hall, where Jasmine called goodbye upstairs to Lily. 'We're off now,' she said.

There was no reply.

'Goodbye, Lily,' Luke called.

'Bye,' Jason repeated, clutching his truck.

There was nothing from upstairs.

I saw them out, then went upstairs to check on Lily. What an afternoon, I thought. Paula's door was closed so I went straight to Lily's room. The door was open a little and I knocked and went in. She was lying on the bed in tears.

'No one loves me,' she cried. 'No one at all.'

'Oh, love,' I said, and went over and sat on the edge of the bed as she cried her heart out.

I now realized it was a mistake having Jasmine and her family come to visit. It had confirmed in Lily's mind that she was alone in the world. I knew she'd suffered abuse in her early childhood, but I didn't know the details.

'Come on, love, dry your eyes.' I reached for a tissue from the box on the table and passed it to her.

'You're the only person who cares about me,' she said, and fresh tears fell.

She was sitting up now, and I put my arm around her. In some ways what she had said was true. I was the only person who cared about her, but I wondered whose fault that was. She'd ostracized those she'd been placed with, including Jasmine – who'd adopted her – and Maddison's Hostel. She'd had no support and no one to look out for her. I knew there were many young care leavers who felt as she did. Some of them go off the rails and never get back on again, leading a life of drink, drugs and poor mental health, sleeping on the street and being grateful when there was a bed in prison. But I didn't want to see Lily go down that path. She was young and had her whole life ahead of her, if only we could get her on the right track. It was going to be hard work, but I felt I could manage it.

'It'll be all right,' I said. 'I know you've had a rough start to life, but so have many young people.' I wiped another tear from her face. 'Do you want to tell me about any of it? Lucy, my other daughter who lives with her partner, had a bad start in life too.'

'Not as bad as mine,' Lily said, blowing her nose and feeling very sorry for herself. 'It was horrible, dreadful. Sometimes I wake up in the night and I'm back there, right in the middle of it. I can't remember a lot of it, but every so often something flashes before my eyes and I wonder if that's what I suffered. I can't remember, but I know there was an uncle Tom who I stayed with. He was horrible. He made me do things to him that I can't talk about, not even to the therapist.' She shuddered. 'It's all such a mess.' Another tear slipped down her cheek, and she wiped it away.

'Lily, if you stay here with me, I want you to see a therapist.'

'No,' she said adamantly. 'I won't.'

'Why not?'

'They're useless.'

'If you find the right one then she might be able to help you. If you don't like her, you can ask for a change.' Although I knew there was a long waiting list to see an NHS therapist.

'I'll go once,' she said, determined not to like whichever therapist she had.

'Good. It may take a while, and I've been thinking: you're eighteen now, so have you ever thought of applying to the social services for your records?'

'My what?' she asked.

'All those years you were in care, the social services would have kept a record of every visit or phone call that was made until you left Maddison's. It would give you a better understanding of your past. But it isn't a decision to be taken lightly. There will be a lot in your records that you won't recognize and some stuff you won't agree with. Some of it will make you very angry and upset. Think about it. You can apply at any time to the social services for your records; they will be held in the area where you were last in care. I'm guessing that was Maddison's.'

'I think so, but I don't know where the other areas were. We moved around a lot.'

'It shouldn't matter. Maddison's will be enough.'

She looked around, then said, 'I don't think I want to know.'

'No, that's fine. Now I think we need to concentrate on the present. So, you definitely want to stay here with me?'

She nodded. 'Where else would I go?'

'If you're staying then I want you to do something: get a job or enrol in college.'

'I'm no good at college work,' she said quickly.

'I know there are access courses run at our local college to allow you in to higher education.' There was also the Open University, but I couldn't see Lily studying in her bedroom.

'I guess I've got to do something with my life,' she said, and shrugged.

'Yes. The other thing that concerns me is Steve Walters. We live not far from him.'

'He goes back to live at university after the Christmas break,' she said.

'That's good, but I don't want you to contact him at all. It will lead to trouble.'

'But supposing I'm pregnant?' she asked.

This seemed to have gone from a certainty to a supposition.

'I suggest we walk to the supermarket shortly and buy a pregnancy test.'

She didn't reply.

'In about fifteen minutes,' I said. 'I need to see Paula first. You can put that jacket on for now. We'll have a look for some clothes too.'

'I don't like this jacket,' she said. It was at the foot of her bed, screwed up in a heap.

'It will keep you warm.'

She pulled a face. I left her to get ready, and went out and knocked on Paula's bedroom door.

'Come in,' she called.

I went in and, before I had a chance to speak to tell her that Lily would be staying for now, she said, 'I know that Lily will be staying. You've got that silly look on your face.'

'Am I really that easy to read?' I said, and smiled again. I went over and hugged her hard. 'Thank goodness I've got you,' I said.

CHAPTER TEN

A NEW YEAR, A NEW BEGINNING

It was nearly 3 p.m. by the time we left the house, Lily carrying the jacket I'd lent her and wearing the T-shirt and trousers she'd arrived in, which I'd washed but they were very thin. I'd found her some jumpers from my supply box that fitted but she didn't like them so refused to wear them. I decided not to say anything further. I knew she didn't like the jacket, but we would hopefully buy another one in the supermarket.

'It's very cold today,' I remarked as we walked up the road.

I could see her teeth chattering. After a while she put on the jacket and left it wide open at the front. I still didn't say anything. Had she done it up she would have been much warmer, but I was learning that this was typical Lily.

We walked quickly along the High Street to the end of the road, where a large supermarket had been recently built. There'd been an uproar when the council had first suggested it, but now most people appreciated it being there. Once inside, I went straight to the pharmacy and found the row of pregnancy testing kits. I picked one up and read the instructions. It seemed straightforward. You just weed on the test stick and the result was instant. Some of them worked before you'd missed a period. According to Lily she'd missed two. I put one in the basket and then we headed for the clothes section. Lily was fiddling with her phone the whole time, texting or scrolling through.

'Are you going to have a look at the jackets?' I asked her.

'They haven't got anything I like,' Lily said, without raising her head from her phone.

I thought this was ridiculous; there were rails and rails of warm jackets and coats.

'Can't we go somewhere else?' she said, still looking at her phone.

'Not today, no,' I said firmly. I continued to walk through the section with coats and jackets, parting the hangers for a better look.

'This one is nice.'

She pulled a face and continued on her phone. I stopped where I was.

'Lily, if you are not going to even look at the coats and jackets then we'll go home now.' I was thinking about the result of the pregnancy test rather than buying Lily a jacket.

'OK,' she said grumpily, and began looking gloomily through the rails of jackets. I guessed she was preoccupied with the thought of the pregnancy test too.

As she was looking, I saw someone I knew so we said hello and had a quick chat. When I looked I saw Lily was now trying on a jacket.

'I'll have this one,' she said.

'Will you wear it?' I asked. It was expensive and I

needed to buy more clothes for her, but if she went to college I assumed she would receive a bursary, although I knew it wouldn't be very big. If she was pregnant then I wasn't sure what we were going to do. Without me realizing it, Lily had become my problem.

'I guess so,' she said. Which I'd learnt meant yes for Lily.

I put it in the basket. She then chose a jumper, the first she came across, a pair of leggings, some underwear and socks, and stuffed those in too.

'I'm hungry,' she said as we passed the food section. 'I'll have a chocolate bar.'

'I think you need a sandwich first. Which one do you want?'

With a stroppy look on her face, she picked up a cheese sandwich and threw it into the basket.

'Now choose a chocolate bar if you like,' I said.

She spent more time choosing one than she had her clothes and was going to open it before I'd paid for it. 'I would put it into the basket,' I told her.

She glared at me, then threw it in. I nearly said something but stopped myself. This girl had a lot of problems.

She followed me to the electrical section, still playing on her phone, and there I picked up another charger.

'Is that for me?' she asked, looking up.

'Yes.'

'That's great. I won't have to use yours any more.'

It seemed the charger meant more to her than the clothes. I guess priorities have changed since I was her age.

We went to the checkout, where I paid. Outside, Lily asked if she could wear her new jacket as it was heaps better than the one I'd given her – she'd already taken off my one. I gave her the new one and she put it on.

'Very smart,' I said.

But she was engrossed in her phone again.

Having eaten the chocolate bar, she threw the wrapper on the floor. I picked it up, but she didn't seem to notice. We began towards the house. The air was even colder now than it had been on the walk to the High Street. Lily was still on her phone. As we neared the house my thoughts returned to the pregnancy testing kit at the bottom of one of the bags. I thought that Lily's life hung in the balance and I was very worried. If she was pregnant, big decisions would have to be made.

Once indoors, Lily took off her new jacket and dropped it onto the floor in the hall, then grabbed the phone charger and ran upstairs. I sighed and picked up the jacket, then I took the bags into the living room. I rummaged for the testing kit and read the instructions again. The test worked by detecting the hormone human chorionic gonadotropin (HCG) in the urine. I wondered if Lily had done one before.

Paula came down and asked me if I wanted a cup of tea.

'Thank you, love,' I said.

As she went into the kitchen I took the pregnancy testing kit upstairs to Lily. She was on her phone but stopped the call as soon as I entered her bedroom.

'Yes?' she asked demandingly, putting down the phone.

I didn't say I hoped the call wasn't to Steve.

'Here we are,' I said, passing her the test. 'Have you done one of these before?'

'Of course,' she said, as if I'd just arrived from another planet.

'So you know what to do?'

'Yes.'

'I suggest you do it now then.'

'I will!' she said with attitude.

I left her to get on with it and went downstairs to drink my tea and then make dinner. At some point I'd have a chat with Lily about the way she spoke to me, but not yet. We needed to see if she was pregnant first.

I heard the floorboards creak as she went into the toilet, then came out again. I was expecting her to come down and tell me the result, but she went back into her bedroom. I waited for her, but she didn't appear, so I put the dinner in the oven and went up to her room. I was nervous for her. What was I going to do if she was pregnant? Talk to her about her options – whether she wanted to keep the baby or not.

I knocked on her bedroom door and waited, my heart in my mouth. There was no reply. I knocked again and she called, 'Come in.'

I opened the door and looked at her. She was sitting on the bed scrolling through her phone. There was no sign of the test.

'Well?' I asked. 'What is the result?' I felt my heart rate speed up.

She looked up at me. 'The result?' she asked.

Was she having a laugh at my expense?

'Yes. You've just done the pregnancy test, haven't you?' Perhaps she hadn't done it yet.

'Yes. It's in the bin in the toilet.' She returned to her phone.

'So, what was the result?' I asked.

'I'm not pregnant. I started my period last night.'

I looked at her in utter disbelief. 'And you didn't think to tell me?'

'To tell you what? No, why?'

'If you're got a period then you're not pregnant, are you?'

'Some people are, but I'm not.'

She returned to her phone.

'Well, thank goodness for that,' I said, although I was annoyed she hadn't told me she'd started her period. 'Have you got sanitary towels?' I asked her.

'No.'

'So what are you using?'

'Toilet paper.'

'I'll get you some towels.'

She wasn't the first girl I'd fostered who hadn't liked to tell me she was having a period and had stuffed toilet paper into her knickers.

I went into my bedroom and took out a packet of sanitary towels and returned to her room.

'Here you are,' I said and put them on the bed.

'Thanks. I'll put one on now, shall I?'

'Yes.'

She went into the toilet while I went downstairs. I honestly didn't know what to make of Lily. I assumed she'd used toilet paper in her pants for the last year when she'd been sofa-surfing. Most girls her age would have asked for a sanitary towel. But I was relieved that she wasn't pregnant – that was one problem we wouldn't have to deal with.

While I waited for the dinner to finish cooking, I

texted Dave Walters. I thought he should know as soon as possible. *Lily isn't pregnant. Cathy.*

Thank God, came his reply.

I could hear his relief, it was palpable.

It *was* a relief, but the only person who seemed to be taking it in her stride was Lily. I then had a nasty thought. Supposing she *was* pregnant? I hadn't seen the result. I'd just accepted what she'd told me. I went quickly upstairs and into the toilet, where I looked in the bin and found the test there, lying on top. It showed a negative result. I breathed a sigh of relief.

I went downstairs and served dinner. It was a vegetarian casserole, which Lily hadn't had before and said she didn't like, but then she ate it.

'What's for dessert?' she asked as soon as she'd put down her fork.

'Have a look in the fridge.'

She went to the fridge and cut a massive slice of fresh cream cake. I saw Paula look at her, but she didn't comment. Lily loved anything sweet. After we'd finished eating, Paula and I watched a movie on the television. I went up and asked Lily if she wanted to join us but she didn't. She stayed in her bedroom for the whole evening, on her phone.

The next day passed without incident. I took Lily shopping again to buy some more clothes and eventually we got something she liked. Paula went to work. Then it was New Year's Eve and I invited all my family round to celebrate. I spent most of the day cooking. I explained to Lily who was coming, and when I texted Lucy and Adrian I just put, *Lily is here.*

Is she staying for a while? Lucy asked.

Yes, I replied.

I look forward to meeting her.

Adrian wrote, *Is that the girl we had to stay on respite many years ago?*

Good grief. I replied, *Yes. You've got a good memory.*

Lily had been with us a week now and I felt she was less depressed. We were still waiting for a referral letter from the psychiatric department at the hospital, but it was the holiday season. It was true, she spent a lot of time in her room on her phone and I had no idea who she was talking to, but I guessed that was true of many teenagers. Paula often spent the evening in her room too, sometimes using her phone. It was her space. Lily never spoke about her friends, which I found a bit odd. I'd known most of my children's friends very well – from school and from living in the same area all their lives. I'd also got to know some of my foster children's friends when they'd stayed with me for some time and had begun inviting them home to tea and going to their houses. Lily was just different, I decided.

Paula helped get the food ready for New Year, setting it on plates and putting it on the table. There was a lot of it. I always overdo the food and end up throwing some of it away. At 3 p.m. they all arrived, Adrian and Kirsty with their little daughter, Sophia, and Lucy and Darren with Emma and Theo. I doubted the little ones would manage to stay up to see in the new year, and I already suggested we put them to bed here. I introduced them all to Lily. There was a lot of noise; there always is when we all get together. Theo and Sophia were of similar ages.

Interestingly, Lily was in her element now; she was all over the little ones, picking them up, holding and cuddling them. This surprised me and I had to tell her to leave Sophia alone a few times. She was a child who didn't like to be fussed over, like her father. It was the happiest I'd seen Lily since she'd arrived, joining in our celebrations. Everyone chatted to each other. Adrian and Lucy knew not to question Lily about her past, but talked of what she was going to do in the future. She said she was going to college. Good, I thought. Excellent.

We ate around 5.30, putting the fridge and freezer food on the table. Then we played some games with the children. They got very excited and had to sit down for a while, then there were more games with prizes. They began to drop off to sleep on the sofa and their parents carried them up to my bed at around 11 p.m. They immediately fell into a deep sleep. At midnight the adults, including Lily, stood in the living room with the television showing Big Ben and counted down the seconds to midnight. 'Five, four, three, two, one!' We cheered and clapped. Then Emma woke and called loudly for her mummy and woke the others. All three of them came downstairs rubbing their eyes and wondering where they were.

'I think we'll take Sophia home now, Mum,' Adrian said.

'I think we'll do the same,' Lucy said.

I agreed.

'Do you have to go?' Lily asked, not wanting the fun to end.

'Yes, I think so,' Lucy said with a smile.

Paula, Lily and I helped them into their cars with all their bags and waved them off. It was freezing outside.

The roof and car tops glistened with frost. The little ones were nearly asleep by the time they disappeared down the road in their cars. Adrian and Kirsty hadn't mentioned anything about fostering but I knew they had the social worker visiting the following week. Paula, Lily and I returned indoors and looked at the mess. With a sigh, Lily went straight up to her room. There were glasses and plates all over the place and the cat was licking the last of the trifle from someone's bowl. I shooed her off.

'Can we leave the clearing up until tomorrow?' Paula said.

'Yes,' I agreed. 'Good idea.'

Paula kissed me goodnight, said 'Happy New Year, Mum,' and went to bed. I put Sheba into the kitchen and then went upstairs myself.

It was now 1 January and I hoped Lily would be able to take advantage of this fresh start. Her conversation about college sounded very hopeful. A new year and a new beginning, I thought as I climbed wearily into bed and switched off the light, full of hope.

CHAPTER ELEVEN

A CHILD

If Lily was ecstatically happy on New Year's Eve, she was very down on New Year's Day. She stayed in bed for most of it and I couldn't understand why. As far as I knew she'd only had one glass of wine to drink the night before. In fact, none of us had drunk much. I kept going up to check on her. I thought yesterday would have helped her bond with us and that something was bothering her. I asked her repeatedly if she wanted to talk, but she didn't.

'Do you want something to eat?' I said. It was late afternoon and she'd had nothing.

'I'll come down,' she said groggily, rubbing her eyes.

'Are you sure nothing is the matter?' I asked again.

'No.'

She came downstairs, ate the rest of the cream cake from the fridge and returned to bed.

Paula and I had cleared up, and I'd texted my family and friends wishing them a Happy New Year. By the evening Paula and I were exhausted. We sat in the living room with the curtains shut against the night sky, our eyes slowly closing. I had Sheba on my lap and was absently stroking her. Paula dropped off to sleep in the chair.

'Why don't you go to bed?' I said gently to her.

She came to and looked at her phone. 'It's only seven-thirty.'

We sat there for another half an hour. Lily came down for a drink and went up to bed again without looking in on us. I wondered what was going through her head right now.

At 8.30 Paula and I went to bed. There was no point in staying up.

'Night, love,' I said and kissed her.

'Night,' she said, giving me a hug.

I went to Lily's room; her door was slightly open so I went in to say goodnight. She was in her new pyjamas in bed.

'You've got a lovely family,' she said wistfully.

'Thank you, love. That's a nice thing to say.'

'Am I staying here?' she asked.

'Yes, if you want to, until we get something sorted out.'

She thought about this, then said, 'Tomorrow I need to tell you something.'

'All right, not tonight then?'

'No, I'm too tired now. I'd mess it up.'

She gave a small, heartfelt sigh.

I said goodnight and came out; I didn't think any more about it. In my experience teenagers often had things to say that turned out not to be very serious. They just thought they were. At least she wasn't pregnant.

The following day I woke refreshed after a good night's sleep. The first thing I did was to look in on Lily, who was still sleeping peacefully. I then went downstairs and fed Sheba. I heard Paula get up. She was going to work today. She came down for some toast and tea and left the house at 8 a.m.

I was less worried about Lily now, even though she'd been fairly low the day before, which I now put down to the after-effects of New Year. I didn't think she'd try to take her life again, and got on with my day.

I had some Christmas cards that were on holders hanging around the living room. Some were from the children I'd fostered who'd kept in touch. Some were doing very well and put a note in their card to say what they were doing. I knew that card-sending was going out of fashion, but we still received nearly a hundred every year, which was nice. I decided to make a start and take those down, followed by the rest of the decorations. I don't like leaving them up until Twelfth Night. We'd put them up at the beginning of December, so they'd been up for a month already. Sheba had her nose pressed to the glass of the patio windows watching a large blackbird hopping across the grass. The garden looked lovely in spring, summer and even autumn, but not now. It looked forlorn.

I got showered and dressed and collected the boxes for the Christmas decorations from the fourth bedroom and took them downstairs. I began taking down the Christmas cards first, checking to remind myself who they were from. I keep all the cards until the following year, when I replace them with the new batch. While I was working, I thought that when Lily was up we should start our research online for any courses that began in January at our local college. Lily needed to do something. At present she had no qualifications and no job. She was floundering.

Having taken down the cards, which took me the best part of an hour, I began on the artificial Christmas tree. It was always a lot faster stripping the tree than decorating it with the little ones helping. I found some chocolate novelties hiding round the back and put those to one side. Once the tree was empty, I took it apart and put it back into its box. It would go with the other decorations into the loft for next year. Christmas seemed to come around very quickly now.

I heard Lily's footsteps coming down the stairs.

'I'm in here,' I called from the ladder in the living room.

She came in.

'Are you taking the decorations down?' she asked, horrified.

'Yes. I usually do it about now.' To be honest I'd had enough of them. 'Are you going to get a drink and something to eat?'

She went into the kitchen and poured herself a glass of juice from the fridge, then returned to the living room.

'Do you want breakfast?' I asked.

'I'll get something later,' she said.

'I thought today we'd have a look at what the local college is offering for this year. What do you fancy doing?' I climbed the ladder so I could reach the ceiling decorations.

'I don't know,' she said softly, and sat on the sofa. 'There's something I need to tell you.'

'Yes?' I looked at her from the ladder. She looked glum now. Whatever she was going to tell me mattered a lot to Lily. I came down the steps.

'Yes? What is it?' I asked, going over and sitting beside her on the sofa.

She fiddled with the edge of her pyjamas, then looked up.

'I need your help. I can't do this alone,' she said. 'I've tried. I realize that now, and there is no one else to help me.'

'But you'll need to tell me what it is,' I said gently.

She looked around the room for a few moments. I hadn't seen Lily this pensive or sombre since she'd arrived.

'What is it, love?' I asked again, my brain searching for a reason. I knew she wasn't pregnant, so what could it be?

'I have a child,' she said at last. 'She's called Olivia.'

I could feel the air crystallize around me.

'A child?' I repeated.

She nodded.

'Maddison's know and the social services and a friend, but she wouldn't tell anyone.'

'Oh,' I said. 'When was Olivia born?'

She told me the child's date of birth. Lily would have been just sixteen when she gave birth. The child was nearly two.

'That's very young to be a mother,' I said. 'Where is Olivia now?'

'With foster carers. I don't know their address. She was taken from me at birth in the hospital and given to them. I didn't want to see her. I could have done but I thought I could just get on with my life. Only now the social services are going to have her adopted and I won't ever see her again. They've sent me adoption forms to sign, because I agreed to it when she was born, but now I want her back.' She began to cry.

Struth! I put my arm around her. Lily was a mother and no more than a child herself. Little wonder she didn't have any qualifications, I thought. She'd been carrying a child and giving birth at the time. To be honest I didn't know what to do. I'd never been in this situation before. I passed her some tissues from the box on the coffee table and waited for her tears to subside.

'Have you had any legal advice?' I asked after a while.

'No. It won't do any good. The social workers are asking me to sign the papers, otherwise they will go to court and have her adopted without my signature. But I want to try to be a mother to her.' Fresh tears fell. 'That's why I tried to take my life. Steve didn't want me, and I felt I had nothing left to live for.'

'You have everything to live for,' I said gently.

'Will you help me get her back?' she asked.

'I can't promise that, but I feel there is a lot we can do. Where's the letter the social services sent to you?'

'I guess it's at Maddison's or one of the addresses I stayed at.' She blew her nose.

'You haven't got it here then?'

'No. They sent me an email that talked about giving consent.'

'Do the social services know you're here?' I asked.

'No.'

'Show me what you have received from them,' I said.

She delved into the pocket of her pyjamas, took out her phone and showed me the emails the social services had sent.

'I haven't replied to any of them,' she said. 'I thought they would go away.' Her eyes glazed over again.

'We need to tell the social services where you are staying and get the forms sent here. We also need to contact a solicitor who specializes in this type of thing.'

'But I don't have any money to pay for a solicitor,' she said.

'I'm almost certain that you will be eligible for legal aid. But that's a question we will ask.'

'Will I get her back?' she asked.

'I honestly don't know, but we'll see what the position is. I am sure you'll be able to see her. Have you seen her before?'

'Only when I gave birth to her.' Tears formed in her eyes. 'But I have a photograph of her from when she was six months old. The foster carers sent it to Maddison's just before I left there.'

'I'd like to see it,' I said.

She went up to her bedroom and brought down the small shoulder bag she'd brought with her. She took out a photo that had clearly been well thumbed. She turned it round to show me, not wanting to let it out of her hand. It was of a beautiful baby on its back, grinning up at the camera.

'She's lovely,' I said. 'Is this the only photograph you have of her?' I knew the foster carers would have sent more.

'I left Maddison's over a year ago and they didn't know where I was staying.'

'I suggest we phone Maddison's first and ask that the paperwork and photographs they have received be sent here to you.' I knew that there should also have been reports sent by the foster carers on how the baby was progressing. 'Maddison's wouldn't talk to me, but if you speak to them and give them this address then you are entitled to receive what the foster carers have sent to you,' I said.

'Really?'

'Yes.'

'That's good. Shall I get dressed?' she asked.

'Yes, love. I'm glad you've told me and I'll do what I can to help, but I can't promise you will get Olivia back.'

'I understand,' she said.

It was now 11 a.m. I left the ladder in the living room to finish taking down the decorations later. I sent Lily upstairs to wash and dress while I prepared her breakfast. What a start to the New Year, I thought. But having said that, I'm happiest when I can get my teeth stuck into something, and Lily badly needed my help. She needed to see her baby, Olivia.

When she came down she looked at the food I'd prepared, horrified.

'I can't eat all that,' she said.

'Eat what you can. You need your strength. We've got a lot to do today.'

It was a cooked breakfast; she needed feeding up. I sat with her at the table as she began eating, and before long she'd finished. It was a clean plate.

'Good girl,' I said. 'Now we're going to phone Maddison's. I'll get the manager on the phone first. This is our address.' I'd written it down on a piece of paper and now passed it to her.

I brought the phone to the table, pressed speaker and entered Maddison's number. We heard it ring for some minutes and I thought their answerphone would cut in, but a woman picked it up and said, 'Hello?'

'Is that Maddison's?' I asked.

'Who's calling?' I knew they'd be cagey about who and where they were; it was, after all, a young person's hostel.

'It's Cathy Glass. I'm a foster carer. Can I speak to the manager, please?'

'Speaking.'

'Good morning. I have Lily Saunders with me. She is living with us now. She'd like all the paperwork and photographs that have been sent to her from the foster carers regarding her daughter, Olivia.'

There was silence before the woman said, 'Is she there now?'

'Yes.'

'Can you put her on, please?'

I did so, and then mouthed to Lily what she needed to say. The manager said she would have to speak to Lily's social worker before she sent all the reports and photographs.

'When?' Lily asked, clearly quite disgruntled.

'I'll phone them today.'

'You'll need my address then, won't you?' she said tartly.

'Yes, please.'

Lily read it out and then the manager read it back to her.

'Is that everything?' the manager asked guardedly.

'Yes!' Lily said rudely, and abruptly ended the call. 'I hate her,' she seethed. 'She's a fucking cow.'

'Is there a reason why you hate her?' I asked.

'No. I just do.'

I had the feeling Lily would have a problem with anyone in a position of authority.

'I know you're stressed, but it's best to try to keep our dealings with them civil,' I said.

'Whatever you say,' she said, still annoyed.

I got her a glass of water. I knew this was testing Lily's patience – of which she had very little – to the limit.

'Now we need to find a solicitor,' I said.

With Lily sitting beside me, I got my laptop out and looked at local solicitors who specialized in childcare cases. I read through what they said about themselves on their website. After about ten minutes I found one, Mr Stanley at Stanley & Higgins, whose office was a few miles away. Lily wanted me to phone them, not having a clue what to say herself. I did so and the receptionist told me that Mr Stanley was with a client at present and would call back as soon as he'd finished. I left the number of the landline.

With the laptop still open, I began looking at access courses offered by our local college. There was a wide selection, but Lily's mind was elsewhere. She kept asking if Mr Stanley would call soon and did I think Maddison's had spoken to the social worker yet? I said I didn't know. Thankfully Mr Stanley called back half an hour later and I put the phone on speaker so we could both hear.

He began by saying he handled all the firm's childcare cases and asked Lily what her position was. She blurted it all out, although not in any order. She said that the cow of a social worker had taken her baby from the hospital when she was born, and now she wanted her back. That she hadn't seen her child in two years but had one photograph of her. I guess he'd heard similar before, because he kept saying, 'Mmm, I see.'

'What's your date of birth?' he asked her, and she told him.

'And your child's date of birth?'

She told him.

'I will need to see all the court documents so I –'

'I haven't got them,' Lily snapped. 'I haven't got anything.'

'No, but the social services' solicitor will have them. Where are you staying?' he asked.

I pointed to the paper where I'd written the address, and Lily read it out.

'I think the sooner I get this going the better, as you've had the letter advising you the social services are going to court. Do you want to come in and see me tomorrow afternoon?'

'Is this going to cost me?' Lily asked, aggrieved.

'You'll likely be covered by legal aid,' he said.

'For all of it?' she asked. 'Only I know someone who had to pay and they couldn't.'

'Come in and see me tomorrow at 3 p.m. and I'll give you the forms. From what you've told me, I'm sure you won't have to pay.'

'But will I have to?' she persisted.

I shook my head.

'My carer says no,' Lily said.

'Bring her too, if she's free,' Mr Stanley said.

I nodded to say that I could attend.

'Yes. She can come.'

'Good. I'll see you at my office at three o'clock tomorrow. Goodbye.'

'Well done,' I said as Lily put down the phone. 'You handled that well.'

Lily's mobile began to ring. She took it from her pocket. It was a private number, but Lily still answered it. I couldn't hear what the caller said but Lily clearly knew them and was instantly full of rage.

'You can fuck off!' she yelled at the caller and hung up.

'Who on earth was that?' I asked, astounded.

'The bloody social worker.'

CHAPTER TWELVE

EVA BLUNT

'It was your social worker?' I asked Lily in disbelief.

'Yes, and I'm not talking to her. She took my baby and she is an old bat,' she said, fuming.

'She is in charge of your case?' I asked.

'I guess so.'

'We need to talk to her then. She's an important person.'

'I'm not talking to her. She's a cow. I wonder how she got my new mobile number.'

'I expect Maddison's gave it to her.'

'Well, they shouldn't have done. They're as bad as she is.'

I sighed and ignored her bad temper.

'We need to speak to someone at the social services,' I said. 'What's her name?'

'Eva Blunt, but I'm not talking to her, ever.'

The call had been made using a private number, so I quickly googled the social services for the area where Lily had come from and called it on the landline. I asked for Eva Blunt. It was a while before I was transferred.

'Eva speaking,' a female voice said quietly.

'Hello. My name is Cathy Glass. I'm a foster carer. I believe you have just phoned Lily Saunders?'

'Yes.'

'Lily is staying with me, but unfortunately she won't talk to you.'

'I see,' she said. I guess she'd heard this or similar a lot. 'I think it's because you took her baby. Is there another social worker that Lily can be assigned to? We have contacted a solicitor,' I added for good measure.

'I'll have to ask my manager. I've had Lily's case since before Olivia was born.'

'But Lily says she doesn't have a good relationship with you,' I said, labouring the point. I knew it was difficult to get a replacement social worker, especially when they'd been working with the young person for so long and the case was being prepared for court.

'I'll speak to my manager and get back to you,' Eva said. 'I've been trying to get hold of Lily since she left Maddison's.'

'I know. It's not your fault.'

'Let me see what my manager says.'

'Thank you.'

Lily was in a rage by now at the social services and was cursing and swearing. 'She's an old bat, the bloody cow.'

'You're going to have to calm down,' I said as I ended the call. 'You can't keep going off on one every time we deal with a social worker.'

'I'm not talking to her!' she said, still annoyed, so I left it at that. I doubted Lily would get on with any social worker who was responsible for her baby.

Later that afternoon Eva called back on the house phone. It was nearly 5 p.m.

'Is that Mrs Glass?' she asked, quietly spoken as usual.

'Yes.'

'I've spoken to my manager and I'm afraid it will be virtually impossible to change social workers now. We're very short-staffed for one thing, and to be honest I don't think Lily would get on any better with someone else.' This woman clearly knew Lily, I thought.

'No, I appreciate that.'

'She's eighteen, so I will need her signature on the adoption papers or I will have to take it to court, but I hope that won't be necessary.'

'That's the thing,' I said. 'Lily is saying she's changed her mind about Olivia being adopted and wants to try to parent the baby. She'd like to see her as soon as possible.'

'Oh, I see.' There was a pause. 'Can I talk to her, please?'

'I'll try to get her to speak to you.'

I took the phone upstairs to Lily's bedroom, where the door was slightly open.

'Eva's on the phone,' I said, covering the mouthpiece. 'She wants to talk to you. I've told her you've changed your mind and want to parent Olivia, or at least see her.'

'What did she say?' Lily asked.

'She needs to talk to you. You're an adult. Come on, love, speak to her. We need your cooperation. There isn't another social worker available.'

She pulled a face but held out her hand for the phone.

'Yes?' she said indignantly into the phone.

She listened for some time, then said to me. 'What's this address?'

I told her and she repeated it back to Eva.

'The day after tomorrow?' she checked, and then a moment later ended the call.

'She's coming here at 11 a.m. the day after tomorrow. She's going to bring some photographs and the paperwork with her. She's going to set up a meeting so I can see Olivia.'

'Well, that's good, isn't it?'

Lily was looking sad.

'Olivia won't know I'm her mummy, will she?' she asked, having already clearly thought about this.

'I honestly don't know,' I said, although I thought it would be unlikely.

At nearly two, Olivia wouldn't know the difference between foster carers and parents. The average child would have a vocabulary of between fifty and a hundred words. Children are encouraged to say Mummy and Daddy among their first words, but they don't know why. I wondered what the carers had done. I also thought of the people who'd been identified to adopt Olivia. I assumed they'd be told shortly about Lily's change of heart. They would've already invested a lot of emotion in her and now that was on hold. What a horrendous shock, I thought. This adoption had been almost certain.

Lily stayed in her room while I made dinner. I was deep in thought, thinking about Olivia's adoption. When Paula arrived home she went to her room to change from her office clothes, then came down for dinner. Lily joined us. The first thing Lily said to Paula was, 'I'm going to see my child.'

Paula, who took everything in her stride and hadn't been aware that Lily had a child, said, 'Oh, yes?'

'The social worker, who I hate, is going to arrange it. She's coming here the day after tomorrow at 11 a.m.'

'To be honest, I didn't know you had a child,' Paula said, and continued eating.

'I only told your mum today,' Lily said. 'Olivia is nearly two.'

Paula nodded.

'I'm going to have to go to Newcastle to see her,' Lily continued. 'That's what Eva said. It'll be the first time I've seen her since I gave birth. I've told Eva that I want to be her mother.'

Paula glanced at me. I knew what she was thinking: that Lily had a lot of learning to do before she could think of parenting a child.

'Good,' Paula said, having heard most things from foster children.

'I've got a photograph of her when she was six months old,' Lily said. 'She'll be two in a few weeks. I'll show it to you.'

'Thank you,' Paula said.

Lily left the table, ran upstairs and brought down the photograph I'd previously seen, then handed it to Paula so she could see.

'She looks lovely,' Paula said.

'I can't wait to get more up-to-date pictures,' Lily said. 'And to see her.' Standing, she then went to her bedroom while Paula helped me clear the table.

'Is Lily really going to try to get her child back?' Paula asked.

'She says so. Let's wait and see what the social worker says when she visits.'

'But she'll need a flat or somewhere to live and a lot of guidance.'

'There are mother-and-baby units where she could stay for the first year,' I said. I'd had previous experience of other teenage mothers I'd cared for going to them.

'Where is the baby now?' Paula asked, aware of some of the practices of the social services.

'As far as I know with the carers she was originally placed with, but I'm certain the adoptive parents will be on the scene by now. Lily agreed verbally to give up the child for adoption at the start.'

'Oh dear,' Paula said. 'Those poor parents.'

'I know.'

My mind was full that evening and night. I lay in bed thinking about everything that had happened. We had the solicitor's appointment the following day, then Eva was coming the day after. I hadn't started a logbook and I thought I should, more for my own benefit than the social worker's. I reached out of bed and made a note on a scrap of paper. I wondered what Eva would say to Lily when she came. I'd never been in this position before. Lily would be pleased to receive the photographs of Olivia, I thought. From time to time I could hear her moving around her bedroom, then her door opened and she went to the toilet. Putting on my dressing gown, I went round to check on her. She was pacing the room and said she couldn't sleep.

'Just lie in bed and try to relax,' I said.

She did, and at some point she must have dropped off for the following morning she was still sound asleep.

I'd decided to buy Lily some more clothes that morning. I'd already suggested to her that she contact the people she'd stayed with and ask if her belongings were there, but she'd shrugged and nothing had arrived. I was aware that Lily didn't have any money, but I was still hoping that she would go to college once we'd found out what was happening to Olivia. There was a chance she would have to go to Newcastle to see the child. It was where she was originally from and where the baby was, so college was on hold until we'd heard what Eva had to say.

I woke Lily at 10 a.m. and said that we would go clothes shopping that morning, though as before, she didn't seem very interested in clothes. I left her to get showered and dressed and went downstairs. As I looked out of the window I saw a few snowflakes fall. Drat, I thought. I checked my phone for the weather forecast and saw that it wasn't supposed to snow. A few more flakes fell, but then the clouds cleared and the sun came out. Good.

By 11.15 we were both in the car going to the shopping centre and Lily was very quiet. I asked her if she was all right.

She nodded. 'Do you think I will be able to parent Olivia?' she asked me.

She'd obviously thought about this a lot.

'With the right support, yes,' I said. 'But parenting needs all of your commitment and it is very hard work.'

'I don't remember you making it hard work when I stayed with you.'

'Sometimes it was,' I said. 'But I enjoyed it. I think that's the key to successful parenting. Enjoy it. Life suddenly goes by, disappears, and you are left with photographs, memories and grandchildren like me. I think life runs away with you. There is more behind me than in front now.'

'I know what you mean,' Lily said mournfully. 'I can remember staying with you nearly ten years ago. The time just vanishes.'

The atmosphere in the car was gloomy as we pulled into the shopping centre.

'Come on, we're going shopping,' I said brightly. 'No more talk of the past.'

I parked and we got out and went to a large store that sold medium-priced clothes.

'Choose something,' I said. She'd been following me around like a doleful puppy. 'Do you prefer jeans or leggings?' I asked.

'Leggings,' she said. 'Black.'

That was easy. I bought three pairs for £19.99.

'What about these tops?' I asked her.

'It's warm in your house,' Lily replied, but eventually she chose three large sweaters and put them into the basket.

Lily didn't want vests, so she chose some T-shirts to wear under the tops, some socks, knickers and two bras. I also bought a pair of trainers.

'Will you get the money back for all of this?' Lily asked.

'I doubt it,' I said. 'Just make sure you don't leave them anywhere.' I smiled.

'I've got just enough for my phone this month,' she admitted.

'How much is that?' I asked.

'Seventeen pounds.'

'I'll give you some money to cover it.'

'I need to pay it into my bank account. Maddison's set it up for me.'

On the way to the car we stopped off at the bank and I paid sixty pounds into her account.

'That will cover the next three months of your phone,' I told her.

'Thank you so much.'

It was the first time I could remember Lily thanking me for anything, and I thought again of the power of the phone. The worst thing in her life was being without it.

We put the shopping into the car and went back into the centre for lunch. When we arrived home it was gone 1.45 p.m. and we needed to leave at 2.30 for our solicitor's appointment. As we went into the hall I saw that some letters had been pushed through the letterbox. I picked them up. One was addressed to Lily. I passed it to her.

'It's from the hospital,' she said, opening it. 'The psychology department. They've made an appointment for me to see a psychiatrist next week. I'm not going. I don't need it now.'

'Oh, yes, I think you should go to see them.'

'No, I'll think about it,' she said and, stuffing the letter into her pocket, took the carrier bags of clothes to her bedroom.

Lily knew we had to leave the house at 2.30 to get to the solicitor's for 3 p.m., given that there would be traffic. At 2.30 I was ready and waiting in the hall, calling up to her every so often.

'Lily, come on, we need to go now.'

'I won't be a minute,' she said again.

Five minutes passed and I called again.

'I'm going to the toilet,' she said.

I wondered if she was prevaricating about going to the solicitor's. She didn't appear until 2.45, so I knew we would be late. I was in a state. I hate being late for appointments.

Sure enough, we arrived late and Mr Stanley was not a happy bunny.

CHAPTER THIRTEEN

MR STANLEY AND HIS ASSISTANT

Mr Stanley was in his early fifties and dressed in a grey suit with a polka-dot blue bow tie. I'd never used this firm of solicitors before, but they specialized in childcare cases, which was what Lily needed. We were shown into his room by the receptionist and we sat down.

'I thought our appointment was at three o'clock,' he said, looking at his watch. 'It's now three-twenty.'

'I'm so sorry,' I said.

'You appreciate I can only give you half an hour.'

'Yes,' I said, flushing up.

'So, you're Lily Saunders?' he said to Lily.

She nodded.

'Put away your phone,' I told her, as she was starting to text.

She pushed her phone into her jacket pocket and Mr Stanley nodded.

'So, what have you been doing with your life?' he asked her.

'Nothing much,' she said awkwardly.

'You call having a baby nothing much?' he asked, surprised.

'I didn't mean that,' she snapped, annoyed.

'So, tell me all about your baby,' he said, unperturbed. I guess he'd heard and seen similar from other clients.

'You should have said that's what you wanted me to say,' LiIy said, scowling at him. 'I gave birth in Newcastle hospital. The social worker came and took Olivia after two days.'

'Why?' Mr Stanley asked as he wrote.

'Because I didn't have anywhere to live and they made up a lot of stuff about me not being able to parent.'

'Like what?' he asked, looking at her.

'That I couldn't take care of myself so I wouldn't be able to look after her. I was supposed to see her, but I haven't.'

'Not at all?' he asked. 'In two years?'

She shook her head.

'Why was that, Lily?' He made a note.

'Because I thought it would be better for Olivia if I just disappeared. I tried to take my own life six times.' This was news to me.

'Are you still suicidal?' he asked.

I looked at her, and I thought the answer was yes.

'No, I want my baby back,' she said.

'Have you contacted the children's services?' he asked.

Lily hesitated.

'Yes,' I said. 'Eva Blunt is the social worker in charge of Lily's case and is visiting us tomorrow.'

'Good.' He nodded and wrote. 'So, what will you say to her?' he asked Lily.

'That I want to see Olivia and I want her back.'

He nodded thoughtfully.

'Will I get her back?' Lily asked.

'I will need to see what stage the adoption has reached. I will have to apply for all the files from the children's services and read through them carefully. I take it the baby is being looked after by foster carers?'

'Yes,' Lily said.

'Do you know if the baby has moved home at all?'

Lily looked at me.

'Not as far as we know,' I said. 'We'll know more after we've seen the social worker.'

'You're Lily's foster carer?' he checked with me.

'Yes. I looked after her ten years ago for two weeks and she arrived on my doorstep on Boxing Day night. She's been staying with us since.'

'That's nice of you. You're not getting paid, I take it? Lily doesn't have a job?'

'No.'

'Now, to legal aid,' he said. 'I take it you'll be eligible as you have no job?'

She nodded, and I said, 'Yes.'

'When you've finished here you can talk to my assistant, who will guide you through the process online. It's important we file the application straight away or I won't get paid.' He laughed and I smiled, but Lily sat there expressionless.

'We understand,' I said.

'So, Lily,' he said, looking at her. 'You will know a lot more once you've seen your social worker. I wouldn't make an enemy of her. I will be in touch with the Newcastle social services for their files. Is there anything you want to ask me?'

'Will I get Olivia back?' Lily said.

'To be honest, it took you a long time to decide you wanted to keep her – nearly two years. Thankfully, as far as I can see the case hasn't gone to court yet. Had she already been adopted, I'm afraid there wouldn't have been anything I can do. Why did you wait so long to change your mind?' he asked.

She thought and then said, 'The staff at Maddison's told me to get on with my life.'

'What's Maddison's?' he said.

'It's a hostel for kids like me. I left it a year ago and was sleeping rough until I came to Cathy's.'

'What brought you all the way south?' he asked.

'Steve,' she said.

'Steve is your boyfriend?'

'No. Just someone I used to know. Then I remembered Cathy and I came to her.'

'Lucky Cathy,' he said dryly, looking at me. 'So, I can put your address down as Lily's permanent home?'

'Yes,' I said.

A buzzer sounded and he glanced at his phone.

'You know that if she's allowed to see her child she will have to go to Newcastle?'

'Yes,' I said.

'Good. I think that's everything. I have a client waiting outside who is on time. I'll buzz my assistant, Gordon, and tell him you're ready to complete your legal aid forms. Please wait in reception.'

'Thank you,' I said, and stood.

Lily stood too.

Outside his office, Lily was seething.

'Idiot!' she said under her breath. 'Wanker.'

'Lily!' I cautioned her. 'Stop it now.'

A young man in a suit was walking towards us.

'Miss Lily Saunders?' he asked her.

'Yes,' she said.

'I'm Gordon Thomas. I will help you with your legal aid application today. This way, please.'

I thanked him and we followed him into a small office, where we sat on one side of the desk and he sat on the other. He logged in to his computer and began by asking Lily for her full name and address and date of birth. He typed, then said, 'These are care proceedings?' and typed some more.

We were there for an hour and a half, although most of Lily's answers were negative. She had no income and no savings, apart from the sixty pounds I'd just paid into her account. She had an email address, although she didn't use it much, and gave him the address. Surprisingly, Lily knew her National Insurance number. They wanted to know virtually everything. Eventually we finished and she was asked to sign part of the form online. I could see that, having sat there all that time and having to behave herself, she was in a bad mood, although, of course, it was for her benefit. As we were leaving, she asked Mr Thomas how long it would all take and was told it would be about three weeks to a month to process her application, and she'd be emailed.

'I may as well kill myself,' she said, once we were outside the building. I'm sure it was a joke, although I didn't think it funny and I told her so.

Once we were in the car I asked her about the previous attempts on her life – she'd mentioned six to Mr Stanley. Children and young people often find it easier to disclose in the car while I'm occupied with driving, rather than in a one-to-one at home when I'm looking at them. I was mindful that before we'd left to see Mr Stanley Lily had said she wasn't going to see the psychiatrist, or rather had said, 'I'll think about it.' She needed to go.

'What of it?' she said, still in a bad mood.

'How many times have you tried to do it?' I asked.

'I dunno – about six, I think.' The last time was when she arrived at my house.

'Why?'

'Lots of reasons, I guess. I don't want to talk about it.'

'No, but you need to see the psychiatrist next week and talk to her or him about it.'

She didn't reply and was scrolling through her phone.

It was obvious she wasn't going to talk to me, but I sincerely hoped she would attend the therapy session the following week and talk to them.

'Which day is your appointment on?' I asked.

'Dunno.'

'When we get home perhaps you can check on your letter and I'll give you a lift there,' I said.

There was no reply.

Once home, I waited for her to go upstairs to her bedroom, which she did straight away, then after a minute I went up after her and knocked on her door.

'Yes?' she said.

I went in. She was scrolling through her phone.

'The letter from the psychiatrist, where is it?' I asked.

'I don't know,' she said, not looking up.

'Can you find it, please?'

She glanced around the bedroom. 'I don't know where it is,' she said.

I then spotted it screwed up in the bin. I took it out. She glared at me.

'I'm not going,' she said. 'I've told you.'

'Why not?' I asked. 'We all need someone to talk to sometimes. The psychiatrist will be good at dealing with problems.'

She didn't reply.

'I'll put it in my diary and give you a lift,' I said and took the letter downstairs.

I wrote the time on the correct page in my diary. It was at 11.30. If anyone needed to see a psychiatrist, it was Lily. I'd now started to think that if she'd already attempted to take her life six times in the past then she could again. It was very worrying, and to be honest I realized I didn't know her or what she was capable of. Her mood could switch in an instant from being reasonably happy to being down and very angry, when she turned in on herself. I was still thinking about this as I began the dinner.

Once Paula arrived home, we sat at the table in the extension to eat. Lily seemed to enjoy the spaghetti bolognaise; there was a clean plate. After dinner both girls went to their bedrooms. I found a book and a pen and began to write a logbook. I thought back over the previous week to when Lily had arrived on Boxing Day night. I wrote a paragraph for each day on what had happened, just enough to remind me should it be necessary. I ended with that day, stating that we went shopping that morning, then saw Mr Stanley and his assistant in the afternoon for advice about Olivia. We'd applied for legal aid and Lily's attitude had been variable, which I thought summed it up.

I put the logbook into a lockable drawer in the front room and took the hoover out from the cupboard under the stairs. Eva was coming tomorrow morning, and although the girls spent most of their time in their bedrooms I gave the room a clean.

I then switched on the television and Paula appeared. I'd heard her come downstairs.

'Hi, love,' I said. I'd got used to her spending most evenings after work in her bedroom. 'Is everything OK?'

She sat beside me on the sofa, and I turned the volume to low.

'I want to tell you something,' she said.

'Yes?' I asked. Paula was a very private person and didn't share a lot. I wondered what on earth it was.

'I've met a guy at work and I'm going out with him for a drink.'

'That's lovely,' I said. 'Wonderful. So, tell me about him.'

She laughed. 'He's thirty-five and hasn't been married before but he has lived with someone. He's about five foot ten and I think he's good-looking. But he's very shy. He finished with his last girlfriend in August, that's the one he lived with, and he asked me if I'd like to go for a drink with him.'

'That's great,' I said. It crossed my mind how freely Paula gave me information compared to Lily. 'I hope you have a nice time.'

'We'll go straight after work. I'll still take my car to work, as I'll just have one drink.'

'Or I can come and collect you?' I offered.

'I'll be fine.'

'What's his name?' I asked.

'Liam Brenan.'

She stood and gave me a kiss, then returned upstairs. Well, that was good news, I thought. She'd been working for the same firm since she'd left college. I knew she'd had other boyfriends in the past, although not that many. I sometimes said she was too choosy, and that she could go out for a drink with someone if they asked. She had some long-standing close friends, though, which was nice.

I was still thinking about Paula when fifteen minutes later Lily came down for a drink. She came into the living room.

'We're seeing Eva tomorrow,' she said.

'Yes, at 11 a.m.'

'I'll try to stay nice and calm and not get angry with her,' she said.

'Good.' I looked at her and smiled. 'I'm sure you'll be fine. Listen to what she has to say, think about it and then respond.'

'I'll try.'

I thought, realistically, the chances of that happening were pretty remote, but it was nice of her to say she'd try. She'd obviously been thinking about it.

CHAPTER FOURTEEN

EVA'S VISIT

The following morning Paula changed her clothes three times before she was satisfied. She kept coming to me and asking me what I thought. I liked each outfit and told her so. She left the house wearing the first one and looking very smart and attractive.

'You look good,' I said as I waved her off at the front door. 'Have a nice evening.'

'Thank you.'

Lily was up early too.

'I couldn't sleep,' she said, coming into the kitchen. 'That old bat Eva was on my mind all night. I kept going through what she would say in my head. I couldn't shut her out.' I could hear her voice rising.

'Calm down, Lily,' I said. 'It's only eight-thirty. Do you want some breakfast?'

'No, I don't. I couldn't eat a thing,' she said loudly.

She poured herself a glass of juice, which she took to her bedroom.

The forthcoming appointment with the social worker didn't stop me from eating. I had two slices of thick wholemeal toast with butter and marmalade. I then checked my email. There was the usual junk, which I deleted, plus a reminder for the foster carer training I was due to give on Monday. It was a talk about safeguarding, for which I'd already prepared the notes. There was also an email reminding me to apply for more outreach work, which I didn't think I could do until Lily was sorted. I emailed them back with a brief explanation of the situation.

Lily came downstairs at 10.30 and sat in the living room, breathing deeply.

'They taught me to do this at Maddison's when I was angry,' she said. 'It makes me feel calmer.'

'Good.'

She got up after a few minutes, breathing forgotten, and walked around the living room, then she went into the front room where she stayed. I went in after her.

'Can you come and sit down,' I said. 'Practise your deep breathing in the living room.' She was in a right state now.

'No, I can breathe in here,' she said, gulping in air.

I sighed and came out. She stayed in the front room until 10.55, when I heard her yell, 'She's here! She's getting out of a taxi. She's got a big suitcase with her.'

She ran into the living room, which is at the back of the house, and sat in an armchair, still breathing deeply. She made me feel nervous too.

The doorbell rang.

'You answer it,' Lily said anxiously.

'Stay calm,' I told her. 'Breathe deeply.'

I went to the front door.

'Hi, are you Eva?' I asked.

'Yes,' she said in the same quiet voice I'd heard on the phone. 'Are you Cathy?'

'Yes. Come in.'

She came in and automatically took off her shoes. I pointed out the slippers she could use in the hall and she put them on.

'It's cold out there,' she said. 'I've booked the cab to take me back to the station in an hour. Here are Lily's things from Maddison's.'

'Thank you,' I said. 'We'll leave the case in the hall. Go straight down. Lily is in the living room.'

I felt my heartrate increase as Eva approached the living-room door. I knew how much this meeting meant to Lily. She was already wound up.

'Hi,' Eva said, in the same quiet manner.

I didn't hear a reply.

'How are you?' Eva asked. 'We haven't seen each other for a while.'

Lily shrugged.

Eva sat down and I offered her something to drink.

'Could I have a coffee, please? No sugar.'

'Do you want something, Lily?'

She shook her head.

I went into the kitchen and a few minutes later I heard Lily explode with anger. I stayed where I was. Eva had known Lily a lot longer than I had. I couldn't hear what she'd said to provoke her, but I heard her say, 'Calm down and listen to me. We'll talk.'

By the time I'd made the coffee, arranged some biscuits on a plate and carried them into the living room, Lily was sitting there agitated but listening. I put Eva's coffee on one of the small tables within her reach.

'Do you want Cathy to join us?' Eva asked Lily.

'Of course,' she said quite fiercely.

I sat on the sofa to listen. Eva sipped her coffee before she opened her briefcase and took out some photographs. She handed them to Lily.

'Some of them had been sent to Maddison's, then after you left the carers sent the rest directly to me.'

Eva sat in silence sipping her coffee as Lily looked at the photographs. There were about a dozen of them, with a little writing on the back of each one. She looked at each picture, then turned it over to read what the carer had written. She went through them quickly first, then more slowly, savouring each one.

When she got to the end she asked Eva, 'Can I keep them?'

'Yes, they're yours,' Eva replied.

Lily passed them to me to look at. They were of a beautiful baby girl who grew with each photograph. The carers had written a few words about Olivia's age and development on the back of each one. 'I have a video too,' Eva said, and she rummaged in her briefcase and took out a memory stick, which she handed to Lily.

'We'll look at it later,' I suggested.

'Yes. I'm only here for an hour,' Eva said. 'I have some of the monthly reports on Olivia's development. Would you like to see them?'

Lily nodded.

I handed the photographs back to Lily, who began going through them again as Eva put the paperwork on the table.

'I've left a suitcase from Maddison's full of your belongings. It's in the hall,' she said.

Lily was too busy looking at the photographs to reply.

'Thank you,' I said.

Eva waited a few moments, then asked Lily, 'What are your present plans?' She took another sip of her coffee.

'Plans?' Lily asked, looking up.

'Yes. What are you going to do?'

'I want to see Olivia.'

'Then what?'

'I want to parent her if I can.'

Eva spoke slowly and quietly. 'You realize that Olivia was placed with the carers she is with now straight from hospital, with a view to them adopting her? She calls them Mummy and Daddy. I collected her from the hospital and took her to them.'

That answered the question that Mr Stanley had raised about Olivia moving foster carers. She hadn't. This was even sadder than I'd imagined. Those poor carers, I thought.

Lily didn't reply. She was studying the photographs.

'Lily, you are entitled to see Olivia,' Eva said. 'I can arrange it, but you should know that the carers are devastated, and Olivia won't call you Mummy.'

'Well, it wasn't my fault,' Lily blurted out. 'You shouldn't have taken her. I want my baby back. We saw a solicitor yesterday.'

'I'm aware of that,' Eva said calmly. 'Olivia is growing into a nice child. Shall I set up a meeting for you to see her next week then?'

I saw Lily hesitate, then she said, 'Yes.'

Eva wrote a note of this.

'I shall be with you during the contact, and it will be held at the centre in Newcastle. I'll email you the details. Is your email address the same?' She read it out.

'Yes.'

Eva made another note. 'Do you have any questions, Lily?' she asked.

Lily shook her head.

'What have you been doing for the last year?' she asked.

'This and that. Then I came to Cathy's on Boxing Day. I can stay here.'

Eva wrote again.

'So, you're not working at all?'

'No.'

'Where have you been sleeping for the last year?' she asked.

'Mainly on friends' sofas.'

'What brought you here?'

'A guy I met,' Lily said. 'I'm not seeing him any more.'

'And how have you been, generally?' Eva asked.

'OK, I guess.'

'No more attempts to take your own life?' Eva asked.

I looked at Lily. 'Maybe a couple,' she said.

'You know that if you put yourself forward to parent Olivia, we'll have to apply for your medical records?' Eva said.

Lily shrugged and stared at the photographs.

I thought it was time I spoke. 'Can I just say that Lily tried to take her life the day after Boxing Day. She told the solicitor that she had done it six times before.' I couldn't sit here and say nothing. It was too important.

'What do you want to say that for?' Lily yelled at me.

'I'm aware of the attempts on her life while she was at Maddison's,' Eva said.

'She has been given a follow-up appointment at our hospital to see a psychiatrist,' I said. 'But she is saying she won't go.'

'No, I didn't,' she said rudely to me. 'I said I was thinking about it.'

'How long have you known Lily?' Eva asked me.

'Apart from two weeks ten years ago, when she stayed here on respite, not long. Since Boxing Day.'

She nodded and made a note. Her phone then rang and she checked it.

'My cab is here,' she said. 'Is there anything else you want to ask me?'

She looked at Lily, who said nothing.

'I'll be in touch about when you can see Olivia,' she said. 'We'll see how it goes.' She put away her notepad and pen. 'Are you sure you don't have any questions?' she asked Lily.

'Which day will I see Olivia?' Lily asked.

'I don't know yet,' Eva said. 'It will depend on the availability at the contact centre.'

'But it will definitely be next week?' she persisted.

'Yes.'

We saw Eva to the door and as we did, Sheba came out of the front room.

'Oh, you've got a cat,' Eva said. 'I love cats.'

She bent down to stroke her, then she straightened. 'I'll be in touch,' she said to Lily. I let her out and closed the front door.

'I love cats,' Lily said, mimicking her. 'What the fuck!'

'She was just being nice,' I said. 'Don't take on so.'

She pulled a face.

'Can we look at the videos on the memory stick?' she asked me.

'Yes,' I said. I knew that Lily would want to see them straight away.

'I'll get your laptop,' she said, and immediately disappeared into the front room.

She took it through to the table in the kitchen extension and switched it on.

'In future, I'd like to be the one to see to my laptop,' I said.

'Whatever you like,' she said tartly.

'And, Lily, can you please try to talk to me in a nicer manner? I'm getting fed up with being moaned at the whole time. I'm doing my best for you.'

'I don't moan at you,' she said.

I wasn't going to get into a 'yes, you do, no, I don't' situation, so I didn't respond. I don't think she knew when she was doing it sometimes. It was her way, and she needed to change. I reminded myself she was young.

The laptop had loaded and she inserted the memory stick into the port. I saw that there were a lot of short videos on it. Lily pressed the first – it was a clip of a baby. 'Three days old', it was entitled, so I guessed it was when they'd just taken Olivia home. The next was a clip entitled 'Two weeks'. She'd already grown. She was lying on her back on the sofa, and her foster father was feeding her a bottle. The next was labelled 'Four weeks'. In the next Olivia was asleep in her foster mother's arms and she was smiling at the lens. And so it continued, a video clip of every stage in her development, just as many parents take now. She was sitting up, rolling over, then there were her first words, followed quickly by her first steps.

Olivia was always smiling – a really happy child – and so were her foster parents. The last clip was taken at Christmas. Olivia was seated on the floor surrounded by presents with the Christmas tree in the background. She looked bemused but happy. I thought no one there could have possibly predicted that the adoption wouldn't be going ahead as planned. As we watched the last video end, there was silence.

'That was nice,' I said at last.

'I'll watch them again,' Lily said, and she sombrely went back to the first video.

'While you're looking at them, I'll make us some lunch. Do you want vegetable soup and a sandwich?'

'Whatever,' she said, poring over the videos.

She didn't go through them in order but this time moved around. I went into the kitchen where I heated the soup and made us some sandwiches. Once they were ready, I took them to the table where Lily was still intently watching the video clips.

'Put the laptop away for now,' I said.

She didn't; she kept looking.

'We can put the videos on your phone later,' I said.

'Can we do it now?' she asked.

'No, your soup will be cold.'

She finished watching the video clip she'd opened and then began on her soup. She hadn't said anything about what she was viewing, and I wondered what she was thinking. It was impossible to tell. We ate in silence, then I said, 'A penny for your thoughts, Lily?'

She shrugged, then said, 'It should have been me in those videos, not them. I should have been the parent instead of those two dickheads.'

'Getting angry isn't going to help,' I told her.

'Well, I should have been,' she said, annoyed. 'If Eva and the rest of the social services had time to support me and my baby, it wouldn't have ended like this.'

CHAPTER FIFTEEN

DOES SHE LOOK LIKE ME?

I didn't know how much truth there was in what Lily had said, and after the outburst she flounced up to her bedroom, leaving her lunch unfinished. I decided to give her some time and finished my lunch, then I went upstairs. Her door was slightly open and I went in. She was sitting on her bed, looking at the printed photographs.

'I hope Eva finds a day at the centre quickly,' she said. 'I need to have a relationship with Olivia. She's too into those two on the video clips.'

They are – or were – her parents to all intents and purposes, I thought but didn't say.

'I suggest you come down and finish your lunch, then we'll upload the videos to your phone,' I said. 'And unpack the suitcase from Maddison's.' She was still looking at the photographs.

'Would you like to put those pictures into a frame?' I asked.

'No, everyone can see them.'

'What about a small wallet for photographs?' I suggested.

'How big are they?'

'About six inches by four inches. They are made to fit the size of those photographs.'

'Yes. That sounds good. We'll get it now.'

'Have your lunch first and then we'll walk to the High Street and you can choose one.'

She followed me downstairs, still holding the photographs, and finished her lunch.

'It's only one o'clock – can we upload those videos to my phone,' she asked, 'before we go to the High Street?'

'Yes, of course.'

She had her phone in her hand. I went into the front room to a drawer containing USB cables. I found one that I thought would connect my laptop to Lily's phone, took it through to the table and plugged it in at both ends. It worked. I'm always surprised when technology cooperates with me. The videos took a while to transfer to her phone and at the end I asked Lily to check they were all there. They were. I was about to delete them from my laptop, but Lily stopped me.

'Can you keep them on there for now? I might lose my phone,' she said.

'Not if you're careful,' I said.

'I've lost three others already.'

I closed my laptop without deleting the photos.

'Can we go to the High Street now?' she asked. She was like a child in her requests, insistent and determined. Everything needed to be done straight away.

'OK. We'll go now. Put on your jacket,' I said.

A few minutes later we were ready to go. Lily was still clutching the photographs. They were all the same size, so I suggested she just took one with us. She returned upstairs to leave the rest in her bedroom. Sheba followed us out of the house but I took her back.

'She'll get lost,' I explained to Lily, who was looking at me oddly. 'She'll follow us into town and not know how to get back. It's happened before.'

We walked up to the High Street and to Boots, the chemist. I found the photography section. There was a display of albums, some of them the right size for what Lily needed. There were about six of them with different pictures and patterns on the front. They had plenty of pockets inside to accommodate all the photographs. There would be some to spare. She took a while choosing an album and checked it for size by sliding in the photograph she'd brought with us.

'Lovely,' I said. 'It looks good.'

She was still hovering by the display, picking up an album and putting it back, then picking up another before returning to the first. I waited patiently. After a while I said, 'Come on, that one looks good.'

She didn't move but remained where she was, indecisive and studying the albums. We'd been there for about a quarter of an hour, and I wondered if Lily was like this in all the decisions she had to make.

'I'll get this one,' she said at last, and put the one she was holding down and picked up one she'd looked at previously.

'Good choice,' I said, and we made our way towards the cash desk.

Lily then ran back and swapped the album she was holding for another one. It crossed my mind then that she might have a condition like ADHD (attention deficit hyperactivity disorder), or was it her past that made her so indecisive? I had no idea, and with no access to her educational records it would remain that way.

I paid for the album, then we left the shop and Lily put the photograph she had brought with her into the album. I went to the supermarket and bought some groceries we needed. I got more than I would have done if just I had been carrying the bags, as I asked Lily to carry one. It wasn't heavy, but she moaned about it constantly on the way home. I swapped bags with her, but halfway she realized that mine was heavier so she swapped them back. We were nearing the top of our road when a woman came towards us.

'Shit,' Lily said, looking at her. 'Shit.'

'Who is it?' I asked.

'Steve's mother.'

As we passed we looked at each other but continued on. Then the woman stopped and came back.

'Excuse me,' she said. 'Are you Cathy?'

'Yes,' I said, fearing the worst, my heart fluttering.

'I'm Mrs Walters, Steve's mother. Hello, Lily. How are you?'

'OK,' she said and looked away.

'That's good. I wanted to wish you all the best for the future. Bye, love.' She smiled.

'Bye,' I said. Lily said nothing to her.

We continued towards home.

'Old bat,' Lily fumed.

'She seemed very pleasant,' I said.

'No, she's not. Why do you always think people are nice? She's horrible.'

'Thankfully you don't have to see her again,' I said, and we continued home.

Once in, I made us both a hot chocolate, which I took into the living room where Lily was. She had finished putting the photographs in date order into the wallet and was looking through them. I looked at them too and admired them.

'When do you think Eva will let us know when I can see Olivia?' she asked.

'I honestly don't know. I'm sure it won't be long.'

'I bloody hope not.'

The reports Eva had brought with her on Olivia were on the table and I picked up the top couple. 'Is it OK if I look at some of these?' I asked. Lily was still absorbed in the photograph wallet. She nodded.

The reports had been photocopied and they were in date order, beginning with Olivia as a baby. Each one was signed by Holly Bowman, the female carer. They were about Olivia's growth and development, the milestones she'd reached. As I read I could see Holly's enthusiasm for her foster daughter shining through. Lily picked up one report, read a couple of lines and put it down again. 'I'll look at them later,' she said. 'Let's unpack the case.'

She was already on her feet, heading down the hall. I put the reports to one side and finished my hot chocolate. It was a large case, but I doubted it contained any surprises. It would have been packed by a staff member at Maddison's. As Lily came into the living room, dragging the case behind her, Sheba shot behind the sofa.

'What's the matter with her?' Lily asked.

'She's scared of suitcases. I don't know why. Perhaps she had a bad experience with one before she came to us.'

Lily opened the case. There were a lot of clothes and toiletries, and some make-up. In an envelope were some more photographs of Olivia, taken when she was less than six months old.

'I'd forgotten I had those,' Lily said, looking through them. 'I'll have to rearrange the wallet. They need to go near the front.'

She put them on top of her photograph album and continued rummaging through the case.

'Oh my God!' she cried, as she neared the bottom. She pulled out a mobile phone. 'I've got a spare now. Great!' It was the most excited I'd seen her.

There were some papers from school, which she wasn't interested in. I suggested we take the case up to her bedroom, where she could unpack it.

'Clothes that you have outgrown or don't want, put in a pile and I'll take them to the charity shop,' I said.

I closed the case and Lily helped me take it upstairs into her bedroom. She'd brought the photographs with her.

'Are you going to unpack?' I asked as she sat on the bed.

'No. I'm going to put all the photographs in the correct order.'

'I'll be downstairs if you need me.'

She nodded, and began taking out all the photographs from the wallet and laying them on her bed.

I went downstairs. I wanted to run through my notes for the training I was giving on safeguarding on Monday. I'd given the course six months ago and twice a year for about six years. I always run through the notes beforehand. After I'd done that, I made dinner. Paula wouldn't be in until later as she was seeing Liam after work.

When dinner was ready I called Lily down. It was macaroni cheese with salad and warm French bread.

'The cook used to make this at Maddison's,' she said, turning it over distastefully with her fork.

Yet she ate most of it and again I was pleased. She needed to put on some weight, but I thought she seemed to be eating just enough. I encouraged her to eat, but that was all I could do at her age. Once Paula's meal was cool, I put it into the fridge and cleared everything away. Lily had gone straight to her room, taking a slice of cake with her. I assumed she was on her phone, probably not texting or phoning, but scrolling through goodness knows what, which personally I think is a waste of time. She spent hours occupying herself doing this, just as many do.

At about 7 p.m. I was in the living room and the landline rang. It was Kirsty.

'I thought I'd let you know how our social worker's visit went,' she said.

Oh dear. I'd forgotten they'd had their first visit from the social worker about fostering.

'Sorry. I would have phoned you, but I've been busy,' I said.

'Don't worry. Are you free now?'

'Yes.'

'We had to put Sophia to bed before the social worker arrived. They don't like little ones up to begin with. She was very pleasant but was with us for over two hours. Based on this meeting, she will decide if she is going to put us forward to foster. I think she will.'

'That's great. What questions did she ask?'

'She wanted to know about our families and background and why we wanted to foster. That took us about half an hour. Then she looked around the house and in the garden to make sure it was suitable for foster children. I explained we had recently moved and were still doing it up. We showed her the foster child's bedroom, which she said was fine. We need to put safety glass in the door from the kitchen to the living room, but apart from that, everything seemed OK. We've got smoke alarms.'

'Good.'

'She then asked us about any experience we'd had with children. I said I was a teacher and you were a foster carer and you'd been doing it for ages. I couldn't remember how long exactly and neither could Adrian. He said he grew up with fostering and you were still doing respite.'

'That should help your application,' I said.

'Yes, she made a note. We'll have to provide references and of course there are the DBS checks, which will be fine. She will visit us again in a month. In the meantime, she's left us both with lengthy application forms. We asked all the questions we'd written down. She said we would be invited to attend some training before our application goes to panel in about nine months. I think that's it, really. There was a lot to think about. We went to bed exhausted.'

'I bet you did,' I said, with a laugh. 'That all sounds very positive.'

We chatted for a while longer, then we said goodbye. It was now 8 p.m. and a few minutes later I heard the front door open as Paula let herself in.

'I'm starving,' she called from the hall, taking off her shoes.

I went into the hall.

'How did it go?' I asked.

'Good. I had a nice time. We're seeing each other again on Saturday. We're going to the cinema.'

'Great.'

'I'm just going to change my clothes,' she said, and disappeared upstairs.

I put her dinner in the microwave, and once she was ready she brought it into the living room to eat. She seemed very happy, which made me happy too. Paula had periods of being low and at one time she'd had a course of therapy. I'm relieved she seems to be recovering now.

That night I looked in on Lily before going to bed. She'd had a wash, but she was awake, sitting in bed thoughtfully, holding her photograph wallet open on her lap.

'All right, love?' I asked quietly.

She nodded.

'I've been thinking, you haven't got any money of your own, have you?'

She shook her head. 'Not a bean.'

'Are you entitled to any benefits?' I asked.

'I don't think so.'

'I suggest you give the social services a ring tomorrow and ask them.'

'OK, but I won't get anything.'

'I'll give you twenty pounds tomorrow to tide you over for now. You need something. I've paid for your phone.'

She nodded. All the while I had been talking, she'd been going through the photographs she held on her lap.

'They're lovely pictures,' I said.

'Do you think Olivia looks like me?' she asked suddenly, clearly having given this a lot of thought.

I'd seen the similarity when I'd first looked at the photographs but wasn't sure if I should say so.

'Yes, I do,' I said.

Her expression changed to one of anger. 'How can those two carers think they can pass her off as their own then?' she demanded.

'They won't,' I said. 'Olivia will be told she is adopted from very early on. As soon as she understands.' I knew that adoption practices had changed over the years.

'How can you say that?' she continued. 'I'm sure she won't be told! I'm certain they will pretend she's theirs. But that's not going to happen. I'll get her back for sure.'

CHAPTER SIXTEEN

UNOBTAINABLE

I sat down with Lily and tried to explain the adoption process with her, but she wasn't interested. She kept repeating that I was wrong and I didn't know what really went on, and that she was sure some adoptive parents lied to their children and brought them up as their own, and the children only discovered their true parentage by finding their original birth certificate by accident. In the end I let the matter drop. I'd said my bit, and it hadn't done any good.

'Night, love,' I said, standing.

Lily didn't reply so I came out of her bedroom and went to Paula's room to say goodnight to her too. She was trying on outfits for her date to the cinema on Saturday evening.

'You can spend all day Saturday trying on your wardrobe,' I joked.

'I probably will.'

I hugged and kissed her goodnight.

'Night, Mum,' she said, smiling.

'Night, love.'

I showered and got into bed and I slept well. It was now Friday, and I wanted Lily to phone the benefits office to see if she was entitled to anything. However, she got up in a very bad mood. How anyone can be in a bad mood when they first wake beats me.

'That stupid social worker hasn't set up contact yet!' she complained, coming downstairs. It was 10 a.m. 'I'm going to phone her now.'

'No, love, I wouldn't. You only saw her yesterday. Wait until next week, then phone her if you still haven't heard anything. She knows you're waiting.' I didn't think she'd advance her case by yelling at her social worker.

'I'll phone her this afternoon then,' Lily said. 'That'll give her this morning to organize it.'

'Before you do that, can you phone the benefits office, please?' I knew she had to make the call because she was eighteen. They wouldn't talk to me.

'Why? I'm not entitled to anything. I've told you already,' she said angrily.

'So you said, but we don't know that for sure, so phone them, please.'

Annoyed, she grabbed the house phone in the kitchen, then glared at me and said, 'What's their number?'

'I'll find out,' I said calmly, and googled the number on my phone. I read it out.

She entered it, then waited. 'It's an answer machine. Do you want me to wait?'

'Yes, please.'

She waited for another couple of minutes, then ended the call. 'I'll try again later. There's no one there.'

'Here's the twenty pounds I said I'd give you.'

'Thanks,' she said begrudgingly. 'I wish I had my own money. Shall I get a job?'

'Yes. What do you want to do?' I asked. 'Something part-time so we can find you a college course as well?'

'I don't know. I haven't got any qualifications. Cleaning or shop work, I guess. I'll look online.'

This was progress, I thought.

Lily spent the next few minutes looking on her phone at jobs with the agencies.

'There are loads of cleaning jobs,' she said. 'It won't be a problem.' And that was it. She put her phone away.

'Are you going to apply for one now?' I asked hopefully.

'I need to phone that stupid social worker first and find out about contact.'

Having forgotten that she was going to wait until this afternoon, she put her mobile on speaker and called Eva's number. I didn't say anything. A series of clicks followed the operator's voice and then a recorded message told her that Eva had the day off and she'd be put through to a colleague.

The colleague answered.

'When's Eva back?' Lily demanded rudely.

'Monday.'

Furious, Lily hung up.

The day passed. I reminded Lily about her hospital appointment on Tuesday. She didn't reply. Then I told her that on Monday I would be out for most of the day giving a training course for foster carers.

'OK,' she said. 'I'll phone Eva while you're out.'

That weekend went by like most others. Lucy appeared on Saturday afternoon with her two children and stayed for about an hour. I'm always pleased to see them, as is Paula. Paula played with the little ones; Lily looked in for a while. The children were very entertaining. They weren't staying for dinner and once they'd gone I made us our dinner, then Paula began to get ready to go out.

'I wish I was going out,' Lily moaned to me. 'I haven't been anywhere in ages. Do you think I can go with them? They're just going to the cinema.'

'No, and please don't ask Paula,' I said.

'Why not?'

'It would put her in the position of not knowing what to say.'

Lily flounced up to her bedroom, where she remained for the evening.

It was then I realized she hadn't called the benefits agency again. It was too late now. I found that I had to remember what she was doing as well as what I had planned. I wrote a note for Lily saying she had to phone the agency on Monday while I was out. Then I watched a movie on television. Lily didn't want to join me and spent the evening in her bedroom.

Paula came back at 11 p.m., having had a lovely time.

'We went for a coffee after and talked and talked,' she said. 'I'm going to see him next week – not sure which day yet.'

'Good. That's nice.' We hugged. I was pleased for her.

On Sunday Paula, Lily and I wrapped up warm and went for a walk in the country. Lily needed a lot of persuading to go but came in the end. She said she'd be bored staying in all day. I don't know if she enjoyed it or not. It was difficult to tell with Lily. There is open countryside not far from my house and we walked for about an hour and a half. Then we returned home and had a late lunch.

On Monday I got up as usual. I should have guessed that Lily was planning something beyond phoning Eva and the benefits office: she was up very early – the earliest I'd seen – saying she couldn't sleep. It was 7.30 a.m. I made her breakfast, which she ate, then she asked me what time I would be going to my 'fostering thingy'. I said 9.30, as it was due to start at 10 a.m. She returned to her room. Before I left I took the note up to her.

'Your lunch is in the fridge,' I said. 'Here's a note on what you need to do today.'

I was expecting an angry retort, but she said, 'Thank you,' very politely. 'I'm phoning about a cleaning job,' she said.

'Excellent. Will you be all right here all day? You have my mobile number?'

'Yes, of course.'

I went out of the house feeling that we were finally making some progress.

The training course went very well. I saw some familiar faces, which was lovely. We chatted through the half-hour lunch break and again at the end of the afternoon. At 4.30 p.m., half an hour after we'd finished, I finally left the council offices. I was feeling good and wondered what progress Lily had made. She wasn't a bad kid, and I hoped in time she would sort herself out. I'd left my phone on silent during the day but had checked it at lunchtime and as we'd finished. There were no messages or missed calls, no notifications that I needed to be aware of. I got into my car and drove home. It was just after 5 p.m. when I arrived.

'Hi, Lily,' I called as I went in.

There was no reply, but that wasn't unusual. Paula wouldn't be home for another half an hour, and I assumed Lily was in her bedroom. She would be lying on her bed scrolling through her phone or fast asleep. She had got up very early this morning, after all.

I went through to the kitchen. Sheba shot in through the cat flap and I fed her, then I filled the kettle for a cup of tea. I couldn't hear any noise coming from upstairs and thought again that Lily must be asleep. I decided to go up and check on her, just to make sure she was all right. I wondered what progress she'd made with the job hunting and phoning the benefits office.

Her bedroom door was closed. I knocked on it gently but there was no reply. I knocked again and went in. She wasn't in there and the curtains were still open against the night sky. I assumed she'd gone out to buy something with the twenty pounds I'd given her. The bed was unmade, but she never made her bed, and the suitcase wasn't unpacked yet. As far as I could see, she'd just taken the small handbag she'd arrived with.

I returned downstairs and checked the fridge. She'd eaten her lunch but had left the empty plate in the fridge. I took it out and then began to make dinner. It would be a quick one tonight: chicken fillets, chips and peas. All the while I was thinking of Lily and where she might be. She didn't have a front-door key. I'd decided not to give her one yet. Perhaps she'd gone out and then realized that. Was she locked out? I decided to phone her mobile.

I left what I was doing, picked up my phone and pressed her mobile number. I was answered by a message saying the number was unobtainable. That was odd, I thought. Why was her phone unobtainable? Perhaps there was something wrong with the network. I tried again with the same result.

Once dinner was in the oven, I tried to call Lily's phone again but I still got the same unobtainable message.

Paula came home and I told her: 'Lily isn't here,' I said. 'I've been giving a training course today.'

'How did it go?' she asked.

'Good. But where do you think Lily is? She hasn't got a key and her phone is unobtainable.'

'I don't know, sorry,' Paula said. 'By the way, I'm seeing Liam tomorrow straight after work. We are going to get something to eat.'

'That's sounds good.'

I boiled the peas, switched off the oven and served dinner. I put Lily's on a plate for when she arrived home, which I still thought she would.

'I wonder where she can be,' I said absently as we ate.

'I honestly don't know,' Paula said. 'She hasn't got another phone, has she?'

Then I remembered. She had a phone in her suitcase upstairs.

'I won't be a minute,' I said.

I put down my knife and fork and went upstairs into Lily's bedroom, where the suitcase was lying on the floor. I lifted the lid and began taking out all her belongings one by one and shaking them. She hadn't made any attempt to unpack the case. It had been left as it had arrived. I took everything out, right to the bottom, then checked the inside pockets. There was no phone there. She must be using that one, I thought, and I didn't have the number. Worried, I returned downstairs.

'You were right. She has another phone that still has credit on it. She must be using it. I haven't got the number.'

I picked up my knife and fork and began eating slowly, all the while wondering what Lily was up to. Why had she taken the other phone? Because she didn't want me to call her?

We finished eating and Paula helped me clear away. I put Lily's dinner in the fridge. Paula then went to her bedroom to relax while I went into the living room and sat on the sofa, deep in thought. I was tired from giving the full day's training and now I had the worry of Lily going missing. Would she come back? Of course she would. All her things were here. But where was she?

I was on tenterhooks all evening thinking of Lily and wondering where she was. It was 9 p.m. when I called our local hospital and asked for Lily Saunders. I waited, my stomach churning and my nerves frayed. When reception came back on the line and said, 'I'm sorry, we haven't got anyone by that name here,' I was relieved.

'Thank you,' I said.

I couldn't phone every hospital in the country, and if she'd tried to take her life again why take her other phone with her? It didn't make sense.

It crossed my mind to contact the police and report her missing, but I hadn't exhausted all possibilities yet and I doubted the police would spring into action.

'When did you expect her home?'

'I don't know.'

'How long have you known her?'

'Two weeks.'

If she didn't come back tonight, then tomorrow I would call Eva. I went up to Lily's room again and checked all her belongings. She was wearing the clothes she'd arrived in and hadn't taken any of the new outfits I'd bought. They were in the bags in her wardrobe, apart from the warm jacket, which she seemed to have taken. I returned downstairs and sat in the living room. Paula came down and looked in.

'Isn't Lily back yet?' she asked.

'No. She hasn't taken anything from her room either. Just the phone and the jacket I bought her. I've phoned the hospital and she's not there. Let's hope she's back tonight.'

'Could she be at Steve's?' Paula asked.

'Wouldn't they have called me?'

'I don't know,' Paula said, and went into the kitchen for a drink. She was used to teenagers disappearing and then returning.

I picked up my mobile and found the Walters' number.

'Hello, Dave Walters speaking,' Steve's father said.

'I'm sorry to call you so late. It's Cathy Glass. Lily isn't with you, is she?'

'No. And Steve has returned to uni now.'

'Thank you,' I said, and hung up the phone.

I sat on the sofa until midnight, then put Sheba to bed, shut the kitchen door and went to bed myself. I would hear Lily if she returned and rang the bell. I lay in bed with my bedside lamp on, thinking and listening, for over an hour, then I must have dropped off to sleep.

I woke with a jolt at 5.30 a.m. and immediately got out of bed and went to Lily's bedroom. Needless to say, her bed was empty. I returned to my room, put on my dressing gown and went downstairs, where I opened the front door to check the porch. That was empty too. Where the hell was she?

I tried her phone her again, but it was still disconnected. Feeling anxious, I went through to the kitchen. Sheba was still in bed and I'm sure would have looked at her wristwatch if she'd had one.

'I know, I'm early,' I said to her.

She slowly got out of bed, stretching as she came over, then immediately began meowing for food. I fed her and made myself a coffee, which I took through to the living room, where I put on the light and sat down. It wouldn't be light for another two hours yet. I sat there thinking. I couldn't imagine where Lily was and vowed to phone Eva at 9 a.m.

CHAPTER SEVENTEEN

CONTACT

I was getting dressed when Paula left the house to go to work. She called up, reminding me she was going out to eat after work that night.

'Bye, love,' I returned. 'Have a nice time.'

I couldn't expect her to share my worries about Lily.

At 9 a.m., dressed and downstairs but still not having had any breakfast, I picked up my mobile and called Newcastle social services and asked to speak to Eva Blunt. She was at her desk and took my call.

'Hello, Eva. It's Cathy Glass.'

'How are you?' she said quietly.

'OK, but Lily has disappeared. I was out of the house all day yesterday giving a training course to foster carers. When I got home there was no sign of her. She didn't leave a message but did take her lunch from the fridge. The phone she's been using isn't working. She's taken the one that was in the suitcase you brought, and I don't have the number for it. I'm not sure if I should report her missing to the police or not.'

It went quiet for a moment as Eva thought. 'No. Not yet. I wasn't aware there was another phone in her case.

Let's wait until tomorrow. You have no idea where she can be?'

'None at all. I've phoned the only place she knows here, which is Steve's home – her old boyfriend. I spoke to his father, and they haven't seen her.'

'Has she taken all her belongings with her?'

'No, nothing. She's wearing the clothes she arrived in and a jacket I bought for her. She's got a small bag with her too.'

'It sounds as if she is planning on returning if she's left all her stuff there.'

'I guess so, but I can't imagine where she's gone. She doesn't know anyone here apart from Steve.'

'And she's definitely not with him?'

'No, his father said he'd returned to university.'

'Let's speak again tomorrow morning and decide what to do then,' Eva said. 'I think we call the police then, don't you?'

'Yes.'

I ended the call, then I remembered that Lily had an appointment to see the psychiatrist at the hospital that morning. I checked in my diary and saw it was for 11.30 a.m. I went upstairs to Lily's bedroom and found the letter she'd been sent in the waste-paper basket. I took it out and went downstairs, where I called the extension number printed on the letter. I told them I'd have to postpone the appointment.

'That's very short notice,' the receptionist replied curtly.

'Sorry,' I said, feeling that I shouldn't have bothered phoning.

'We'll send another appointment, but it won't be for a while. This was considered an emergency by the psychiatrist.'

'Sorry,' I said again.

I put down my mobile. I wasn't going to give her the full story. I returned to wondering where Lily was and what on earth she was doing. Part of me said that I didn't think she'd try to take her own life again, but you can never be sure. Every time I heard a noise at the front of the house I went to see what it was. I even opened the front door a few times to check the porch, but Lily wasn't there.

I made a piece of toast and ate it sitting on the sofa in the living room and staring out through the patio windows at the desolate winter garden. My mobile rang. It was from a private number, but I answered it.

'Is that Cathy Glass?' Eva asked.

'Yes. Hello, Eva.'

'I thought I'd tell you that Lily has turned up safe and well.'

'Thank goodness,' I said, and let out a huge sigh of relief.

'But she's in trouble. She went to the home of Holly and James, Olivia's foster carers.'

'Oh no. How did she know where they live?' I asked.

'A friend of hers is a looked-after child who by chance lives in the same road as Holly and James. The parents know each other and, having checked Olivia's birthday with Lily, she put two and two together. Lily went to Holly and James's home this morning and told them that Olivia was hers.'

'Oh no.'

'As you can imagine, they are very upset and not sure what to do. I'd set up contact for Thursday where I was going to be present, but I'm going to see Holly and James later today.'

I didn't know what to say. I was grateful Lily was safe and well, but what was she going to do now? 'I have all her belongings here,' I said.

'She might return to you. I just wanted to let you know she'd been found.'

'Thank you.'

We hung up and I felt a mixture of relief and disappointment.

The rest of the day passed without incident. Paula arrived home at 10 p.m. having had a lovely time. She told me a bit about Liam, where he lived and what he looked like, but said it was 'early days yet'. I was hopeful this would lead to something.

'When do I get to meet him?' I asked.

'Not for a long time!' she exclaimed. 'I've only been on three dates with him.'

That night I lay in bed thinking of Lily. I wondered where she was sleeping. With a friend, I guessed. I woke at 7 a.m. just as Paula was getting up. I picked up my phone from the bedside cabinet as I do most morning and was surprised to see three missed calls from Lily's number at around 5.30 a.m. I always sleep with my mobile on vibrate. She must have swapped her phones back, I thought.

I sat up in bed and immediately called the number. Lily answered straight away.

'How are you?' I asked.

'OK, I guess.'

'What's the issue with the phone? I tried to call you yesterday.'

'I took the SIM card out. I didn't want to speak to you, but that old phone was rubbish, so I put it back.'

'All right.'

There was silence.

'Eva phoned me yesterday,' I said. 'She told me you went to Holly and James's home.'

'I know it was wrong. I only caught a glimpse of Olivia.'

'Where are you now?' I asked.

'In a bedsit that Eva found me. It's horrible. I was going to sleep on a friend's sofa, but Eva said I had to stay here.'

'So what's been going on then?' I asked.

'I've got to go to contact tomorrow at a place in Newcastle.'

'The contact centre?'

'I think so. Holly and James won't be there, just Eva and Olivia, and I wanted to ask if you would come too.'

'Me? But why?'

'You're the only adult I trust.' Which was very sad.

'Have you asked Eva if I can come? Contact is usually only for family members.'

'Yes. She said if I wanted you to be there then you can come if you haven't got anything else on. That's why I'm calling you.'

'What time is the contact?' I asked.

'Two o'clock. I will be very upset and I will need you there. There is no one else.'

'All right,' I said. 'I'll meet you at the contact centre just before two o'clock. What's the address?'

'I don't know. Eva is going to give it to me. I'll phone you when I have it. Can you bring some of my clothes with you? I left in a rush yesterday, on the spur of the moment.'

'Yes. How long are you there for?'

'I don't know. As long as it takes, I guess.'

'I'll see you at the contact centre. If there is any change in the arrangements, please let me know.'

'I will. Thanks, Cathy.'

Her manner was very different now; she sounded far more subdued than usual.

'What are you doing now?' I asked her. I could picture her alone in a bedsit; it was a sad thought.

'Waiting for Eva to phone.'

After we'd hung up, not completely trusting Lily, at 9 a.m. I phoned Eva, who confirmed that I could attend contact at 2 p.m. the following day. She gave me the address and said she was going to see Lily just before.

'Thank you,' I said. 'I'll see you tomorrow.'

I went upstairs into Lily's room and packed a bag. Not the suitcase: that would suggest I didn't want her to come back. I could send it to her another time if necessary. I got her toothbrush and toiletries from the bathroom and packed those as well as some clothes. I put the bag on the landing ready for tomorrow. I was planning on driving to Newcastle in the morning. It would take me around three hours, depending on the traffic.

When Paula arrived home I told her where I was going the next day and why.

'You're a good sort,' she said. 'I'll be fine here. Of course you have to go.'

I left home on Thursday just at the end of the school run at 9.30 a.m. with my sat nav on and sandwiches and coffee on the seat beside me. I'd left Paula's dinner in the fridge for her to heat and told her I'd be back that evening.

Contact usually only lasted for a maximum of two hours, sometimes an hour. On this occasion I hadn't been told how long it would be. As I drove, my thoughts turned, as they often did, to Lily and what she must be feeling – to see Olivia one to one after so long … I also wondered what Holly and James were feeling. Lily had a right to see her child, but the effect it was having on them must be devastating. They'd looked after a child for nearly two years and had assumed she was theirs, and now this.

A letter had arrived the day before addressed to Lily from the solicitor we'd seen and I'd brought it with me. I also had a small overnight bag on the back seat, in case I got delayed. I was hoping to bring Lily home with me after contact but had a bag packed for her, just in case she needed or wanted to stay where she was.

Apart from some road works that slowed me down, the drive went fairly well. I stopped approximately half-way there at a service station to use their toilet and stretch my legs. I returned to the car and had a sandwich and a cup of coffee. Snack over, I resumed the drive. The last part of the journey saw me enter Newcastle at lunchtime. It was very busy and the sat nav took me straight through the centre of town. Although it was only 1 p.m., I decided – not knowing the area – to go straight to the contact centre. I could wait outside if necessary.

Fifteen minutes later I pulled up outside a brick bungalow building. I parked at the side and switched off the engine. I got out, checked I had the correct building and returned to my car to wait. It was a fine, sunny day, although very cold. I had three-quarters of an hour to wait but I didn't want to stray far. I ate the rest of my sandwiches and drank the rest of the coffee from the flask, then texted Paula, who had wanted me to tell her when I arrived. I always tell her not to worry about me, but I know she does.

At 1.30 I saw a car pull into the car park. Eva and Lily got out. I stayed where I was. Eva would want to talk to Lily and explain how the contact centre worked. As they walked up the drive Lily looked very serious. Eva pressed the security bell, the door opened and they disappeared inside. Ten minutes later another car drew up and a woman and a man got out of the front. They were in their thirties. The woman opened a rear door of the car and helped a child out. I guessed she was about age two. Was it Olivia? I stayed where I was. It wouldn't have been appropriate for me to introduce myself, and it might not have been them. The contact centre is used by numerous families, so I couldn't be sure if this was Olivia or not.

The child walked between the adults, holding a hand each. The adults looked serious too, just as Lily had. The man pressed the bell and they were admitted. I waited another five minutes, then at 1.55 I got out of my car and, drawing my coat around me, went up the path and pressed the bell.

'I'm Cathy Glass,' I said to the receptionist. 'I'm here with Eva Blunt and Lily Saunders to see Olivia.'

'Wait there,' she said. 'You can sign in.'

My stomach was churning as I signed the book. I took a deep breath. What must Lily be feeling? I wondered. The receptionist went to the back of the office and made a quick phone call. Eva appeared from around a corner.

'Hello, Cathy. Thank you for coming all this way. I know Lily will be pleased to see you. We're through here.'

I smiled and followed her along the corridor, where I could hear other families playing with their children in the rooms we passed. The centre seemed bigger than the one I was used to. We went into one of the rooms, where Lily was sitting on a chair. As soon as she saw me she jumped up, ran over to me and hugged me hard. I was taken aback; this was so unlike her.

'I'm so nervous,' she whispered. 'Olivia didn't see me yesterday and I only caught a glimpse of her. This is the real thing. Supposing she doesn't like me?'

I would think that at Olivia's age she would wonder what the hell was going on, I thought but didn't say. The contact supervisor was seated at a table ready to take notes.

'You'll be fine,' I said, drawing back. 'But don't be all over her. Let her come to you.'

'Are we ready?' Eva asked. 'Any questions?'

'How long is contact for?' I said.

'Normally it would be for an hour, but we've got the room for an hour and a half today,' Eva replied. 'Olivia's foster parents will be either inside the building or close to it, in case Olivia gets very upset. I've talked to Lily about that. Cathy, I assume you know how to behave in a contact centre.'

'Yes.'

'Are we ready?' Eva said, looking at Lily.

'Yes,' I said, and Lily nodded.

'I'll fetch her then.'

Eva went out of the door and my pulse quickened. I could see that Lily was getting more and more anxious.

'Calm down. Be yourself,' I said. 'And remember to keep it low key.'

'I'll try,' she said, stressed.

It was a good five minutes before the door opened again. I assumed Olivia needed some persuading to come. The door slowly opened and Eva came in holding the hand of the child I'd seen being brought in. She was beautiful, of average height and slightly built, like Lily, with masses of long dark hair and large brown eyes. Lily stood.

'Let her come to you,' I said quietly. 'Remember, this is the first time you've met.'

Eva was still holding Olivia's hand and brought her slowly to us.

'Olivia, this is Lily and Cathy.'

'Hello,' I said with a smile

I didn't know what the child had been told about Lily, but she looked at her with big open eyes.

'Shall we find some toys to play with?' Eva suggested.

She nodded, not taking her eyes from Lily.

Lily and I watched Eva and Olivia sit on the play mat just in front of us. Eva showed Olivia some toys. Olivia wasn't saying much but kept looking at Lily.

'Come and join us,' Eva said to Lily.

Lily gingerly went over to where they were. She picked up a toy house, then put it down again. Olivia was watching Lily intently. I realised then that Lily didn't have a clue how to play with children. I wasn't sure if Eva knew this. It's not natural; we learn how to play from our parents or older siblings who played with us as a child. I watched for a while longer and realized this wasn't going anywhere.

'Lily, why don't you play?' I said.

Olivia looked at me hopefully, then back at Lily.

'Mummy,' she began to cry, over and over again, and tears immediately sprang to her eyes and ran down her cheeks.

CHAPTER EIGHTEEN

LILY AND OLIVIA

Lily stared at Olivia, not knowing what to do with a crying child. Eva put her arm around Olivia's shoulders and soothed her. 'You're all right, there, there,' she said. 'Don't cry.'

The child laid her head on Eva's shoulders, as I was sure she did with her parents when she was upset. I looked at the scene and thought surely it's human nature to comfort a small child who is upset, but Lily sat there, unmoved, and stared at her, almost frightened.

Eva continued calming Olivia and eventually her tears subsided. Rubbing her eyes, she stood and toddled off to the toy grocery shop that appeared to sell almost everything.

'Mummy,' she said again, and looked around the room briefly as if she was expecting to see her mother come in.

Eva stood and went over and began to play shops with her. I knew I was there to observe only, so I stayed where I was.

'I'll have a jar of coffee, please,' Eva said to her, and picked up the small plastic jar and gave it to Olivia.

Olivia put it back into the shop, then looked towards the door, I guessed searching for her mummy again. Her gaze returned inquisitively to Eva, but she didn't say anything. I remembered reading in one of the reports that Eva had left with us that Olivia was on target with over a hundred words. To be honest, the poor child looked terrified. She toddled over to the door and tried to reach the handle but couldn't.

'Come and sit down,' Eva said, and got up and brought Olivia back to the play mat.

Lily was still on the mat but not making any attempt to play with her daughter. She was staring at her with a blank, frozen, almost hostile expression. Olivia stood again and continued to wander around the room, going to the door and looking for her parents. I assumed she'd been shown the room when she'd first arrived with Holly and James. At one point she looked up at Eva and said, 'Mummy.'

It could have been a question – was Eva her new mummy? She was behaving like one, a lot more than Lily was. How very confusing for the child.

After about another ten minutes of similar behaviour, I couldn't just sit there any longer and watch the scene, so I said quietly to Lily, 'Why don't you go over and play with Olivia?'

She shook her head but said nothing. She appeared very wary of her child, who was typical of most children her age before life's experiences have set in and was becoming more confident and inquisitive.

After another five minutes or so had passed of Eva playing with Olivia, Eva came over to me and sat down, leaving Lily sitting on the floor with Olivia wandering around. Eva took a notepad and pen out of her briefcase and began making some observations.

'Are you writing about me?' Lily asked quite aggressively.

'No,' she said. A few minutes later she put away her notepad.

Olivia looked at the only person now sitting on the floor – Lily – picked up a toy car and toddled over to her, holding it in her outstretched hand. It was obvious to anyone that Olivia wanted Lily to take the car and possibly to say thank you. I'm sure that's what Holly and James would have done. Olivia went right up to Lily, while she sat motionless, then the car was pushed closer to Lily's face, which was at Olivia's height. Lily jerked back and said in a firm voice, 'Don't do that.'

Olivia stopped what she was doing and her little face crumpled. She began to cry again. Goodness knows what was going through the poor child's mind. I glanced at the clock on the wall. So far, we'd been there half an hour; there was still an hour to go.

'Shall I play with Olivia?' I now asked Eva.

'Perhaps show Lily how it's done,' she said.

I gathered together some of the toys and books and sat next to Lily on the play mat.

'Come on, let's read Olivia a story,' I said to her.

'She doesn't want one,' Lily said.

I opened the top book and began to read. Olivia was still wandering around aimlessly, but then she heard my voice and, being used to stories read to her by Holly and James, she came over and sat on my lap, bless her. She wanted to look at the colourful pictures. While she studied the first picture, I read the few words that were printed on the page opposite, pointing to the illustration.

'There's the bright-green frog,' I said, and I made the noise a frog makes. '*Ribbit, ribbit.*'

She looked at me, then tried to make the noise, but her little face was serious. I did it again and again, and eventually she gave a small smile. Eva smiled too, but Lily just looked at her daughter. I turned the page. There was a picture of a bright-pink pig. I read the few words written on one side of the book and oinked loudly. Olivia laughed and tried to copy the noise.

'Well done,' I said, and clapped.

We oinked for a while longer, then I turned the page again. There was a picture of a horse, so I read the words and neighed loudly. Olivia copied, trying to neigh. I clapped again.

'Well done,' I said. 'Perhaps Lily will do the next one.' I turned the page.

Lily looked at the open book and, possibly from embarrassment, read the words about a cow in a low, flat voice and then said, '*Moo, moo.*'

'*Moooo*,' I said. '*Moooo.*'

Olivia didn't copy the noise and wanted to turn the page again, but Lily had her hand on the book so she couldn't.

'This is a silly book,' Lily said.

It was, but not for a child of two, and once again I thought that Lily might be embarrassed to read it.

The cow was the last picture, so Olivia then got up and went to find another book, but the one she brought back was for older children. It was about space. She brought it over and sat on my lap and opened it. I began to paraphrase it.

'Where's that written?' Lily asked.

'It's not,' I said. 'I've made it up. The writing is too much for a child of two.'

'She's not two for another couple of weeks.'

I continued until Olivia had had enough and then closed the book. She stood and began wandering around the room aimlessly. Eva and I tried to get her interested in something the room had to offer. Usually, children don't want to leave the contact room because of all the toys and activities in there.

'Mummy, Mummy,' Olivia said every so often, and she was soon close to tears again.

The poor child. I think that if Lily had made more of an effort to entertain her, she would have settled, but as it was Lily just sat or stood and couldn't or wouldn't engage with her child, despite Eva and me encouraging her.

It was getting close to 3 p.m. when Eva said to Lily: 'Shall we end the session now? I think Olivia has had enough.'

'Yes,' Lily said, and she stood, ready to leave.

'You and Cathy wait here in the room while I find her parents,' Eva said.

Eva went over to Olivia and, taking her hand, said, 'Let's find your mummy and daddy.'

The child looked up at Eva, wide-eyed. 'Mummy and Daddy?' she asked hopefully.

'Yes, let's go.'

Eva opened the door and we watched them exit, Olivia holding tightly onto Eva's hand. The door was left open and we heard their footsteps receding down the corridor outside, then a voice I took to be Holly's said, 'Hello, my love. You're early.'

'I'll speak to you later,' Eva said and, saying goodbye to them, she returned to us.

She closed the door and we sat down. She nodded to the contact supervisor, indicating that they could go.

'Well, Lily. How do you feel the session went?' she asked.

'Why did you call Holly and James "Mummy and Daddy"?' Lily said bluntly.

'I suppose it was a slip of the tongue,' Eva said. 'I'm sorry if it offended you.'

'Yes, it did. They're not her mummy and daddy,' Lily said aggressively.

'Point taken. So, how did you feel about the session today?'

'It was OK, I guess,' Lily said.

The answer should have been that it was shocking. Lily had made no effort at all to engage with her daughter, even when she'd been upset.

'Do you think you could have done anything differently?' Eva asked.

'No,' Lily said. 'Olivia didn't want to play with me.'

'Do you think you could have played with her more?' she asked. 'I appreciate it was the first time you'd met her.'

'No, I don't. When can I see her again?' Lily asked, regardless of everything that had happened.

'I don't know yet,' Eva said. 'I want to talk to Holly and James first and discuss this with my manager.'

'Why?'

'To see how Olivia is after contact. If we go ahead, I think it's likely to be next week. I'll let you know.'

'Thank you,' I said.

'What do you mean, *if* it goes ahead? I want to see my child and I have a right to.'

'I'm sure you will,' Eva said.

We stood and the three of us left the room. As we passed a closed door on the right I heard a couple talking to their child. I didn't know if it was Holly and James, but it could have been. They sounded so loving and tender, and again I wondered about Lily and her past.

Eva saw us to reception, where we signed out.

'Thank you for organizing this,' I said to her.

'You're welcome. Are you going home with Cathy?' Eva asked Lily. 'Or to the lodgings I organized for you.'

'To Cathy's,' Lily said. 'Last night was horrible.'

'All right, I'll be in touch,' Eva said.

We went out of the main door as Eva returned inside the building.

'My car is over there,' I said to Lily, and pressed the fob.

We got into the car in silence. I had expected a reaction from Lily but there was nothing. It was now 3.20 p.m. so I guessed we'd be home around 6.30; once we were settled, I sent Paula a text message telling her when we'd be home. Lily was scrolling through her phone. She hadn't looked at it during contact, so I assumed that Eva had told her not to.

'I brought a bag of your clothes,' I said as I started the engine, 'in case you needed them, but we'll take them home. And there's a letter from the solicitor we saw.'

She leant over to the back seat, picked up the solicitor's letter and ripped it open as I pressed *Home* on the sat nav. It was a thick letter, and I glanced at her as she read it.

'I can't understand this,' she said, looking at the first page, and threw the letter and envelope onto the back seat.

'I'll look at it once we're home,' I said.

I pulled away and drove for a while in silence. I was deep in thought; Lily was scrolling through her phone. I wondered what Eva was saying to Holly and James.

'Lily,' I said after a while, once we were on the motorway. 'Can you put your phone away? I want to talk to you about something serious.'

She glanced at me. 'What is it?' she asked, still scrolling through her phone.

'When you're ready,' I said, and continued to drive.

I waited and eventually she turned her phone over in her lap.

'What is it?' she asked again – I would have said with attitude, although I'd done nothing to upset her.

'Can you tell me about your early childhood?' I asked. 'What you have been through? I think it has shaped the person you have become.'

She was staring straight ahead now and not making any attempt to answer.

'What is your earliest childhood memory?' I'd asked similar direct questions before to other teenagers I'd fostered and sometimes it produced a direct reply.

'Not having enough to eat,' she said. 'But I told the therapist that.'

'Can you tell me, please? I think it might help me to understand you better.'

'I had a bad childhood – that's all there is to know,' she said tightly, looking out of her side window.

'But what do you mean by bad?'

'I didn't have enough to eat and I was hit repeatedly by a woman I thought was my mother. I hated my life. Then I was taken into foster care and eventually adopted. I remember I played them up a treat. I don't blame them for getting rid of me. I was really horrible. I remember hurting children at school, and when my parents had visitors I'd take the children to my bedroom to play and make them take off their clothes. That's what was done to me. I didn't know any different. I thought that's what you did with visitors.'

I was silent for a few moments, then said, 'But when you came to me ten years ago I remember you soon settled down. I've looked after some very difficult children whose behaviour was appalling, but yours wasn't. I don't understand.'

'I could be two different people if I wanted to be. I guess I held it all in. And we were very busy at your place, so there wasn't time for me to get up to my tricks. I would have done, given the opportunity. I was very, very angry underneath that your children had everything and I had nothing. Anyway, I guess if I'd behaved better, I could have stayed with Jasmine and Luke. They were nice enough. Maddison's was even worse.'

'I thought you wanted to go to Maddison's – that's what Jasmine told me.'

She shrugged. 'I don't know. I was at that age when you rebel against everything that you don't like, and I didn't like any of it. So I slept around and eventually got pregnant. Everyone tried to make me have a termination, which made me even more angry. I know now when I'm angry, but I can't help it. It's got to come out or I'll go mad.' Which I'd heard from other teenagers before.

'And what about your behaviour in contact just now with Olivia?' I asked. She was staring through the windscreen, her face serious.

'I didn't want her to get close to me.'

'What, physically, you mean?'

'Yes, and mentally. If she gets close, I don't know what I'd do. She's my daughter, but I don't know how to love her. I'm not sure I even want to. I'm in a right mess.'

'Have you told anyone how you feel?' I asked.

'Not really.'

'I think we need to tell Eva. It will help her understand your behaviour in contact today.'

Lily thought for a moment, then said, 'If you want to, but I can't change. It will take me a long time before I can even touch Olivia, but I do want to see her.'

She turned her phone over and began scrolling again. I decided to leave it for now. Lily had told me a lot, and it was important I passed the information on to Eva.

'I can phone Eva tomorrow if you like,' I said.

She nodded.

The rest of the drive was a nightmare. There was a bad accident on the motorway that held us up for over an hour. We stopped at the next service station and got something to eat. I texted Paula and told her what had happened.

Take care, Mum, she replied. *See you later x*

We finally got home at nearly 9 p.m. It was pitch dark and I was exhausted. I took the overnight bags from the back seat of the car together with the solicitor's letter. 'Do you want to read this now?' I asked Lily.

'No, you look at it.'

We went inside and Paula came down from her bedroom to greet us. Lily took her bag upstairs and went straight to bed.

'Do you want a cup of tea?' Paula asked.

'Yes, please, love.'

While Paula made the tea I went into the living room, drew the curtains and read the solicitor's letter. It was nothing important – just confirmation of what we had agreed in the meeting and that the legal aid had been applied for. I put it back into the envelope. Tomorrow I needed to phone Eva. Perhaps she would make allowances for Lily's behaviour. From what I'd seen today it was doubtful whether another contact would go ahead other than one for Lily to say goodbye to Olivia for good.

CHAPTER NINETEEN

OLIVIA'S PRESENT

It was getting on for 10 a.m. the following morning and I was waiting on the phone; I had been for ten minutes. I'd tried to phone Eva at 9 a.m. but had been asked to phone back in half an hour, which I was doing now. The woman I'd spoken to asked me to hold or said Eva could call me back. I decided to wait. It was Friday and the social services would be closed over the weekend other than for emergencies. Paula was at work and Lily was still in bed. I'd told Lily last night I was going to phone Eva and she'd said, 'Fine,' but hadn't asked for any details about what I was going to say.

As I waited on the phone I gazed down the garden at the bare trees. One lone blackbird was foraging for food on the lawn. Suddenly Eva came on the phone. 'Hello, Cathy, sorry to keep you waiting.'

'That's OK. I guessed you were busy, but I wanted to talk to you. Lily knows I'm calling.'

'Go ahead.'

'Yesterday's contact was a disaster and on the way home I spoke to Lily in the car. I am sure you already know a lot of this, but she told me she'd had a very abusive childhood.'

'Yes. It's all in the folder.'

'Lily is very awkward around people. She doesn't like touching or being touched. I've hardly been able to get close to her since she arrived. She shies away from me. It's something she needs to explore in therapy. She told me as I was driving that it will be a long time before she can even touch Olivia, but she'd still like to see her. That's all she said. I might be wrong, but I think yesterday was a shock to her and she is starting to realize that for her to parent Olivia it would take years.'

'That's the feeling I got yesterday,' Eva said. 'But we can't wait years. Olivia needs permanency and stability now.'

'No, I appreciate that. I wondered if you'd be setting up another contact. I hope Lily will do better.'

'I'm meeting my manager shortly to discuss this case,' Eva said. 'Holly and James are asking what Lily's intentions are. I've said I don't know yet. It's too early to say. As you can imagine, they are heartbroken.'

'Yes.'

'Is Lily there?' Eva asked.

'No, she's still in bed. We had a bad journey back yesterday.'

'If I set another contact for next week, will you come?'

'If Lily wants me to, which I think she will.'

'I'll speak to Lily on Monday. Was there anything else?'

'No.'

'Have a good weekend.'

'And you.'

I ended the call in the hope that Lily would be able to see Olivia the following week; if so, I would go with her.

* * *

A little while later, Lily appeared in her night clothes, yawning.

'I couldn't go to sleep,' she said.

'No, it was an awful drive back. I've just spoken to Eva and she's going to phone you on Monday.'

'About contact?' Lily asked.

'I think so. What do you want for breakfast?'

'Just a cup of tea. I'll get it.'

'Then come back in here. I want to talk to you.'

While she made herself tea, I took the solicitor's letter from the envelope.

'I thought we'd go through this together,' I said as Lily returned.

'As long as you read it. Have I got legal aid?' she asked.

'It says it's been applied for. Come and have a look.'

She reluctantly sat on the sofa beside me and I held the letter between us.

'How much of the first page can you read?' I asked her.

'All of it,' she replied indignantly, and took a sip of her tea.

'Can you really?' For I had a feeling she couldn't read much of it at all. She'd been in and out of school all her life and didn't have any qualifications. I doubted she could fully read the letter.

'Dear Ms Saunders,' I began. 'Thank you for coming to see me and bringing Ms Glass with you.' I stopped and looked at her.

'What does the next line say?' I asked.

She picked out half a dozen words, but they were unlikely to make much sense to her. Then she suddenly stopped. 'So I'm no good at reading,' she said angrily. 'So what? A lot of people can't read very well.'

'It helps me to know,' I said. 'I'll read it to you, don't worry.'

'That's what I've always done, got a friend to read it to me.'

'Have you ever been diagnosed with anything, like dyslexia?' I asked.

'I've no idea.'

I read out the first page, which was outlining the case. The rest was about legal aid.

When I'd finished Lily asked if she could go to her room.

'Yes, of course. Then, once you're dressed, come down, please. We need to get some structure into your life. Have you phoned the benefits office yet?'

'No, but I need to. It's Olivia's birthday soon and I want to buy her a present. Will you help me?'

And for a moment I teared up. Her request was said so gently and was so heartfelt.

'Of course. Get dressed first, then we'll phone the benefits office together,' I said.

Half an hour later Lily came downstairs, washed and dressed.

'What's the number of the benefits office?' she asked, holding her phone.

I found it and read it out. We had to wait in a holding queue before we were put through. She was eighteen and they wouldn't talk to me unless the claimant was special needs, which as far as I knew Lily wasn't. They took some of her details and said she wasn't entitled to a care leaving grant as she was living with me. She was, however, entitled to universal credit of £300 per month, but she had to apply online.

'Great,' she said, and ended the call.

I fetched my laptop and found the government website on universal credit. There were pages to read about eligibility. Lily soon lost interest and began scrolling through her phone. We hadn't even logged in yet. I stopped what I was doing, sat back in my chair and took my hands from the keypad. I gazed leisurely out through the patio windows. It was a while before Lily noticed anything was wrong. She turned to me.

'What are you doing?' she asked.

'Waiting for you,' I said.

'Have you filled in the form?' she asked.

'No.'

In fairness to her, I don't know how the average person ever completes the forms. There are so many links to follow.

'I want you to put away your phone and look at the forms with me,' I said. 'It's your universal credit.'

'I can't do it.'

'I can understand that, and I'll help you, but I'm not doing it for you. In fact, you can type it.' I thought that with her just sitting beside me there was a great temptation for her to let me do all the work.

I put the laptop onto Lily's lap and she looked at the list of links.

'What do I do?' she asked.

'I'd click on that one,' I said, pointing. She did and there was another link that I read out.

Eventually we found the page where she could begin her application.

'Type your name into that box,' I said, pointing to the screen.

She did, slowly looking at the keypad. I realized she couldn't type either. What had she done at school ...? Then she had to enter her email address, which she knew by heart.

'Now you need to make up a login password,' I said.

She made one up and we wrote it down with a capital letter, seven lower-case letters, three numbers and a sign, but when she entered the password into the website a message said she already had one.

'Have you tried to access this website before?' I asked her.

'I think I might have done.'

'I take it you haven't kept a note of the password you used?'

She shook her head. 'No.'

'We'll have to apply for another one then.'

It was a quarter of an hour before we had actually accessed the website and Lily, always short of patience, was losing it badly.

'This is why I didn't apply before,' she said, hitting a key hard.

'That's not going to help,' I said.

The next question was asking for her National Insurance number.

'I've got that in my purse,' she said proudly, and ran upstairs and brought down the card.

'You always have to keep this,' she said.

'That's right. Who told you that?'

'Someone at Maddison's.'

She typed in her National Insurance number. Then she had to identify herself, either using a driving licence, passport or bank details.

'Have you got a driving licence or passport?' I asked her.

'No.'

But I knew she had a bank account. She found it online and we entered all her details. It said they would verify who she was but that she should continue filling in the form. Her personal circumstances were next.

'What's personal circumstances?' Lily asked.

'Things like health, family responsibilities and financial situation. You're not bankrupt, so type no.'

In fact, most of her answers were 'no' or 'not applicable'.

'Your money will go straight into your bank account, but all correspondence will come here,' I explained to her. 'Is that all right?'

'I guess so. There's nowhere else for my letters to go,' Lily said.

And so we continued, with Lily slowly but surely filling in the pages on the website. It took us nearly an hour to complete the form. A note at the end said it could take up to five weeks for her to receive her first monthly payment.

'Shit!' she exclaimed. 'Five weeks! What the fuck?'

I suppose she'd thought she'd get it straight away.

'You could apply for the interim payment,' I suggested.

'And go through all that again? Not bloody likely! But how am I going to buy Olivia's present?'

'I'll give you something,' I said.

'I'll pay you back,' she said. 'Can we go to the toy shop now?'

I glanced at the clock. It was nearly 12 noon.

'Yes. We'll go to the giant superstore at the shopping centre on the far side of town.' I usually visited it before my grandchildren's birthdays and at Christmas. You can get most toys there. 'It's only a short drive away,' I said, retrieving my laptop from Lily, which I closed and put away.

Lily's anger disappeared and she looked quite happy. She was going to buy her daughter a birthday present for the first time, and my heart went out to her. It occurred to me that if the next contact didn't go ahead then we'd have to post Olivia's present.

I'd never seen Lily get ready so quickly. She ran upstairs, grabbed her winter jacket and was out the front door before I'd finished locking the back door. I came out and we got into the car. She was smiling now and I saw a completely different side to her. She was looking forward to buying her daughter a present; it was something that clearly meant a lot to Lily.

During the fifteen-minute drive she googled the shop on her phone and was looking at their website. She talked non-stop about all the presents she saw on there that she wanted to buy for Olivia's birthday. There were pages of them. After a while I reminded her that Olivia was only going to be two and that some of her present ideas were for much older children. But she continued anyway.

'What about a closed-in trampoline or one of those toy motorcars?'

We parked in the multi-storey and went down in the lift to the shopping centre.

'Where's the shop?' Lily kept asking me over and over again.

'Down here,' I said, and I led the way.

To say she was like a child in a sweet shop was an understatement. She rushed into the store, then up and down the aisles, oohing and ahhing and picking up enticing boxes of toys, especially the very large walking, talking dolls for over eighty pounds each. I decided to give Lily her money so she could budget.

'How about if I give you thirty pounds to buy Olivia's present?' I said.

'That's not much,' she replied, pulling a face. 'I said I'd give it back to you.'

I could see she was overexcited so, ignoring her bad humour, I took thirty pounds from my purse and gave it to her so she could look at gifts that were that price or under. She couldn't make up her mind and a few times I lost her in the aisles. It was a massive store where some of the toys in some of the aisles were labelled with the approximate age range. I wandered around and chose a few small gifts for birthdays, which I then paid for. The store was certainly very tempting.

After about an hour I called to Lily and said we needed to go shortly and she should choose a gift. Another half an hour passed before she came to me holding two reborn baby dolls in boxes. They were gorgeous and so life-like. One was a boy and the other a girl.

'Which one?' she asked.

'They're both lovely. I don't know. You choose,' I said.

Lily stood there looking from one to the other, unable to decide.

'That one?' I said, pointing to the boy.

In the end she chose the girl and put the boy back on the shelf. We went to the checkout, where Lily paid for it.

She had two pounds change. Her excitement had dropped now and I thought it was because she had made her choice and bought the doll. Yet she also seemed slightly worried as we made our way to the exit. We walked out of the store, and as we did so a security guard followed us out and walked straight into our path.

'Can you step aside, please?' he asked Lily.

'I'm sorry, why?' I said.

'I think she may have something on her that she hasn't paid for.'

CHAPTER TWENTY

POCKET MONEY

The blood rushed from my head. I felt dizzy. A second security guard arrived.

'I need you to give us the toy you haven't paid for,' he said to Lily. 'And you're banned from this store.'

Lily stood there bold as brass, facing up to him.

'What if I don't?' she said.

'Then I will have you arrested.'

'You can't,' Lily said. 'Only the police can do that.'

He was about to reply when I came to and said firmly, 'Lily, whatever it is you've taken, give it back now.'

People were starting to stare at us on their way out.

'Now,' I said firmly. 'Now, Lily.' I was feeling hot and sweaty.

She hesitated, then took a small item from under her jacket. It looked like a toy caterpillar with a light. She threw it on the floor. One of the security guards picked it up. It was worth £3.99.

'I'm so sorry,' I said.

'Can I go now?' Lily asked with attitude.

'Yes, but don't come back to this store.'

'I won't,' she said and strolled off.

'I'm sorry,' I said to them again.

I was livid and acutely embarrassed. I quickly walked away and found Lily waiting further along the mall. She didn't seem at all fazed.

'Lily, what have you done?' I asked.

'I tried to take something. It wasn't expensive. The shop can afford it.'

'That's not the issue,' I said. 'Stealing is very wrong. I gave you the money for Olivia's present and you took something else. You were lucky they didn't call the police.'

'Big stores don't prosecute for under two hundred pounds.'

I stared at her, aghast. How did she know that? Clearly she'd stolen before. I felt utterly dreadful, appalled.

We walked in silence to the car. I drove home not knowing what to do. Lily was scrolling through her phone again. I'm not someone who gets worked up easily, but this had really rocked me. A younger child I could excuse. Indeed, I'd fostered children who'd stolen before, but never someone Lily's age – until now.

I drew up and parked outside the house, and before we got out I turned to Lily and said, 'Don't ever do that again.'

'OK,' she said too easily, and got out.

Inside the house, I couldn't rekindle the excitement of Lily buying Olivia's present, although Lily, not caring about the shoplifting, had completely forgotten the episode, or didn't care.

'Are you in the habit of stealing?' I asked her.

She didn't reply, so I thought the answer was yes. I would put my handbag away in future. I'd been leaving it around the house.

'You don't do it when you're living with me,' I said. 'Do you understand?'

She shrugged.

'Do you understand me, Lily? I'm deadly serious. If you bring the police to my door again then that's it, I'm afraid.'

'All right. I heard you. I won't,' she said gruffly. 'I should have pinched some wrapping paper and a card for Olivia while I was in there.'

I didn't respond. She went to her bedroom while I put my handbag in my bedroom, together with the presents I'd bought. I was still reeling from what had happened. It's really difficult when someone who lives with you steals. You simply can't trust them in the house with your belongings. I felt I needed to talk to someone, and a few minutes later Lucy phoned. I wouldn't normally have discussed this with her, but I'm glad I did.

'Hi, Mum. Have you got a sledge we can borrow for the nursery? It's for a winter display.'

'Yes,' I said. 'I'll get it out of the shed. When do you need it?'

'Are you OK?' she asked. 'You sound down.'

'I've just had a really embarrassing incident in the shopping centre and I'm fuming.' I told her what had happened and asked her to keep it to herself, which I knew she would.

'Is Lily going to be prosecuted?' Lucy asked.

'Thankfully, no. But they said they didn't want her in their shop again. I can't go back there either.'

'Oh dear. I'm sure you will be able to in time.'

'I hope so.'

'Do you give Lily any pocket money?' Lucy asked. 'Like you used to do with me and Adrian and Paula.'

'No, I've paid for her phone and the present, and I gave her twenty pounds as a one-off. I buy what she needs, and she's just applied for the government's universal credit, but that could take up to five weeks to come through.'

'I'd give her something, say ten pounds a week, until it arrives. Then she'll have some money of her own for any bits and pieces she might want.'

'Yes. That's a good idea. She hasn't got any money of her own. I'll do it now. Thanks, Lucy.'

'One of the first things you did when I arrived was to give me some money of my own. It was the first time I'd had any and I really treasured it.'

'I remember you used to put it into your money box that Grandma and Grandad bought you.'

'Yes. I've still got it.'

'You used to save up. I think you only ever bought presents with it – either for birthdays or Christmas, or flowers for me.'

'You remember the flowers?' Lucy asked, surprised.

'Yes, of course. I pressed a petal from the first bunch you gave me. I've still got it in one of the books in the front room.'

'That's wonderful,' Lucy exclaimed. 'Can I see it when I get the sledge tomorrow?'

'Sure.'

Lucy made an arrangement to drop by in the morning around 10 a.m. for the sledge and we said goodbye.

I went straight into the front room and dragged a chair over to the bookshelves so I could reach the top shelf. I found what I was looking for easily. There was the petal in an old and very thick book, which I took down and opened carefully. It was a pink rose. It had been beautiful all those years ago and still was now. I gingerly picked it up and looked at it. It was perfectly preserved. I put it back into the book for safekeeping. I had a few others in there too and turned the pages. One was from a bouquet of flowers Adrian had given to me on his graduation and another was a carnation Paula had given to me, thanking me for her eighteenth birthday party. There were a few others whose origin I had forgotten. I closed the book and returned it to the shelf.

Now, what to do about Lily? I wondered. I was less angry now; talking to Lucy had helped. I went upstairs to my bedroom, found my purse and took out a ten-pound note. Lily had never asked for money since she'd arrived and I'd bought everything she'd needed, assuming that would be enough. But as Lucy had said, it was nice to have some money of your own.

I went round the landing and knocked on Lily's bedroom door.

'Yes?'

'Can I come in?'

'Yes.'

I opened the door. Lily was lying on her bed scrolling through her phone.

'Lily,' I said. 'Can I talk to you?'

She nodded and looked up.

'I'm going to start giving you ten pounds a week until your universal credit comes through.' I put the ten-pound note on the bed beside her. 'Now you can buy a card for Olivia. I've got wrapping paper.'

'Thanks,' she said, looking at the money. 'I'll go now,' and jumped off the bed.

I was having to accept that Lily was impulsive and wanted to do everything now. She grabbed her jacket and shoes and headed downstairs.

'There's a card shop in the High Street,' I called after her.

'I know it!' she replied and rushed out, slamming the front door behind her.

I wondered if I should give her a front-door key but decided I'd wait a bit yet.

I went to my bedroom and found suitable wrapping paper in a drawer. I took out a sheet together with the sticky tape and scissors, put them on Lily's bed and came out.

Lily returned after about an hour. I was in the kitchen preparing dinner. I left what I was doing to answer the front door. Lily was standing there holding the biggest card I'd ever seen. It was in the envelope as I doubted there was a bag that would fit it.

'That's huge,' I said as she came in.

'It was reduced from £10.99 to £8.99.'

She excitedly took the card out of the envelope and held it up. On the front was a huge Minnie Mouse in her red-and-white spotted dress. She was smiling at the viewer, her head tilted to one side to look cute. She had her hands clasped together in front of her and underneath her picture were the words *Happy Birthday* in black ink.

'That's lovely,' I said.

Lily proudly opened it and inside were the words *I love you*.

'Very nice,' I said, hoping again that we could deliver the card in person, for there was no way it was going to fit in the post box.

'I've left wrapping paper and scissors on your bed,' I said.

'I'll wrap the present now,' she cried, her excitement palpable.

As she ran upstairs I returned to making the dinner.

Sometime later Lily came down and showed me the wrapped box and the words she'd written in the card.

I love you so much. Love from Lily.

Which I thought was quite appropriate.

'Put it somewhere safe until we hear from Eva,' I said.

She took it back to her bedroom.

Paula arrived home and Lily clattered downstairs again, holding the present and card to show her.

'Very nice,' she said. 'It's a big card.'

'Look at the words I've written,' Lily enthused, and opened the card for Paula to see.

'Lovely,' Paula said.

And again, I hoped we would be able to deliver it in person, because how else was she going to get that card to Newcastle?

The following day Lucy arrived at 10 a.m. to collect the sledge. She was alone. Paula was up and they had a chat, but Lily was still in bed. I'd already brought the sledge out from the shed and had left it on the patio. First, though, I showed Lucy the book in the front room with the pressed flower in it.

'I had no idea you'd kept it,' she said, amazed. 'I told Darren.'

'I bet he thought I was daft,' I said, slightly embarrassed.

'No, he could understand it.'

She asked if I'd given Lily the pocket money and I said I had and that she'd immediately spent most of it on a very large card for her daughter's birthday.

'That's nice. She can spend it as she wants.'

Lucy then said she needed to be off as they had a busy day ahead, so I went out onto the patio and brought in the sledge. She added that the nursery where she and Darren worked were putting on a winter display for the week and she'd return the sledge the following weekend.

'No worries,' I said. 'No snow is forecast.'

I waved her off at the door.

We woke the following morning to a find a thick, white blanket of snow outside.

I had a feeling that something was different even before I opened the curtains. There was a lull, a hush, that muted sound that came from outside. Through the gap in the curtains I could see that everything seemed brighter. I got out of bed and opened the curtains. It was truly marvellous. We didn't get snow very often now, and this was the first time for some years. I guessed it was about three inches deep and covered the rooftops, pavements and people's front gardens. It had clearly caught the council out, as there was no sign of it being cleared.

It was 7.30 a.m. as I went downstairs. Paula and Lily were still asleep. Paula had gone out with Liam the night before and I had been in bed when she'd returned. I assumed the snow hadn't fallen last night or she would have looked in to my bedroom to see if I was awake to tell me.

I opened the kitchen door. Sheba greeted me, purring loudly. I stroked and fed her. She ate about half of her breakfast as she usually did, then shot out of the cat flap – only to shoot straight back in again, meowing loudly.

'It's snow,' I told her.

She was a rescue cat, so I had no idea if she'd seen snow before coming to me. She looked up at me, then decided to finish her breakfast before trying the garden again. I made coffee and toast and opened the back door for Sheba to go out. She stood at the entrance sniffing the air. It was beautiful outside but very cold.

'Come on, make up your mind,' I said. 'It's freezing out there.'

She decided to stay in.

I took my coffee and toast into the living room where I opened the curtains. I admired the white garden. It looked wonderful covered in snow. Like a fairy tale. I put the local news on the television and soon learnt that the snow had travelled down from the North and across the middle of the country, taking us all by surprise. The weather forecast said that no more snow was forecast, but then they hadn't predicted this.

It would be lovely to go for a walk, I thought. We didn't have the sledge, of course, but I could see the top of some of the grass poking through the snow, so I doubted it was deep enough for that anyway. I ate my breakfast, and then got dressed.

At 9 a.m. Paula appeared on the landing.

'It must have snowed in the early hours,' she said. 'There was none when I got home just after eleven.'

'I know. Did you have a nice time?'

'I did, thank you.'

'Let's go for a walk in the snow,' I suggested.

'Yes. I'll get dressed,' she said, smiling. I guess we are all children when it comes to snow.

I woke Lily soon afterwards – it took a while, and when I told her about the snow she didn't share my enthusiasm.

'Nice,' she said and turned over, and closed her eyes.

'Come on, we'll go for a walk. Are you coming?'

I repeated the question and then there was a groggy, 'Yes.'

An hour later the three of us were ready to leave the house. Sheba was indoors now, asleep by the radiator in the living room. We put on our winter jackets, gloves and scarves, and went out. It was great fun being one of the first to walk on the pavement in the snow. Lily was like a small child, avoiding the odd footprint and stepping in the untrodden snow. We walked up the road and through the park where a few children were already out with their sledges. Even though the grass showed through the snow, they still seemed to get up speed on the slope; there was just enough snow to make the sledges go.

We continued walking through to the countryside close to where I live. We were in a line and I was last. I held back and made a snowball, which I threw at Paula, then made another one, which I threw at Lily. She was angry to begin with but then saw the fun in snowballing and returned one.

We were out for three hours before we came home. The temperature had risen towards midday and the snow was beginning to melt.

By the following morning there was nothing left but grey slush. It was Monday and the start of another week.

As soon as Lily got up she asked when Eva would phone about her seeing Olivia.

'She said sometime today,' I replied.

As the morning went on, she grew increasingly agitated and annoyed, asking again and again when Eva would phone. At 11.30 she said she'd phone her if she didn't hear shortly. I told her to wait but she called her anyway. She was told that Eva wasn't in the office that morning. Eva had said she would phone on Monday but hadn't stated a time. Lily's anger grew as the day proceeded. She tried to phone her again at 2 p.m., with the same result. Her colleague asked her if she could help her.

'No, you can't!' she cried bluntly and hung up.

'It won't help if you get angry. If Eva doesn't call today, we'll phone her tomorrow.'

'Tomorrow!' Lily shouted. 'I'm not waiting till then. She said she'd phone me today.'

Thankfully Eva phoned at 3.30 p.m. She called Lily's mobile, and although Lily brought it into the living room to speak to her I couldn't hear what was being said. It was a short call. Once she'd finished, she said, 'I can see Olivia on Thursday again. Will you hand over the present for me?'

'Why me?' I asked, astounded.

CHAPTER TWENTY-ONE

MISSING EARPHONES

'I'm sorry, I don't understand,' I said.

'Will you give the contact supervisor the birthday present and card I bought for Olivia?' Lily said. 'Then they can give them to her parents for her birthday.'

'But why? You can give the card and present to them yourself, surely? What's the problem?' I asked. 'I don't understand.'

She shrugged. 'Nothing.'

'It'll be fine, please don't worry.'

But Lily did worry about Olivia, and about giving her the present and card – big time – and her worry increased with each passing day. I tried talking to her but without any effect. I honestly didn't know what got into her sometimes. We were still waiting for the hospital to reschedule the appointment for her to see a psychiatrist, and I decided she needed something more to occupy her, so I suggested we look at college courses, but she couldn't concentrate. In the end I sent off for literature on foundation courses at our local college. Lily was investing so much energy in Olivia that I wondered what would happen when a decision was finally made about the child's future in court. I didn't dare contemplate it.

Lily didn't go out of the house until Thursday, although I tried to persuade her. She sat in her bedroom, scrolling through her phone and listening to music. On Wednesday evening I told Paula to expect us back tomorrow whenever we arrived, and not to worry if it was late. By Thursday morning I was feeling as nervous as Lily was about contact, which had been scheduled again for 2 p.m. We left the house with Lily barely visible behind the huge card. I carried the present, plus some sandwiches and drinks. I wasn't just going for the ride but to support Lily. She arranged the card on the back seat as I pressed the address for the contact centre on the sat nav. As we left the house Lily put in some earphones, which I hadn't seen before. I didn't say anything, but I wondered where they had come from.

The drive there wasn't too bad and we arrived in Newcastle at 1 p.m. I parked in the same place as I had done before and produced the sandwiches and drinks. Lily nibbled on one but soon didn't want any more and threw it out of the window. Her nervousness increased as 2 p.m. approached. A little before we were due to go in, we saw a car drive up and park. I thought it could be Olivia's foster parents.

As we watched, Holly and James got out of the car. Lily gasped, then Holly lifted Olivia out of the back. Lily looked at her as though in a trance. Holly and James were stony-faced, and it seemed that Olivia didn't want to go inside either. She tried to get back into the car. James had to carry her in. I glanced at Lily, who was still staring at them. She didn't say anything and I wondered what she was thinking. Her right leg had begun to jump up and down – a sure sign she was worried.

'I can't go in,' she said at last.

'Why not?'

She shook her head. 'I just can't.'

'We have come a long way to see Olivia. I think you'll regret it, but it's your decision.'

A few minutes passed, then she suddenly flung open her car door and got out.

'Are you coming or what?' she said to me.

I got out and she took the card and present from the back seat. A strong wind had whipped up, and I had to help her steady the card. We walked to the door and I pressed the bell, the door released and we went in.

'That's a big card,' the receptionist said with a smile.

'We're here to see Olivia,' I said.

'You're in the same room as last week, go through,' she said.

We went along the corridor to the room. The door was slightly open and a contact supervisor was in there talking gently to Olivia.

'Come in,' she called. 'Close the door behind you.'

We went in and Olivia looked at us with big round eyes and grabbed hold of the contact supervisor's skirt. The poor child looked petrified. She'd led a normal life until now, and then she'd suddenly had to come to this unfamiliar building, where she couldn't be with her parents, and play with two strangers. Lily stood there clutching the card and present, and just stared at her.

'Could you give the card and present to the parents?' I said to the contact supervisor. 'It's Olivia's birthday next week.'

'Sure.'

Lily handed them to her and, with Olivia in tow, she tucked them behind the desk she was going to work at. Her laptop was already open on it. She returned to stand in the centre of the room. Olivia dropped the contact supervisor's skirt but kept close to her and was now staring at Lily.

'Let's play with something,' I suggested.

I made my way towards the toys, but Olivia went to the bookshelf and began going through the books. She came to the one that I'd read last week and brought it to me. I guessed she'd remembered – at age two it was likely. I lifted her onto the sofa between Lily and me with the book open between us.

'Would you like to read the story?' I asked Lily.

'No. You do it. You're better than me.'

So I read the book of animals, beginning with the frog – *ribbit, ribbit* – then the pig – *oink, oink* – and continued to the end. When I'd finished the book Olivia closed it, took it back to the bookshelf and got the other one on space out that was too old for her. There is safety in what you know.

I opened the book and began to paraphrase it as I'd done last week. Once I'd read a little, Olivia closed the book and returned it to the bookshelf. She then stood there, looking at us.

'Shall we play?' I asked.

She gave a little nod. I went over to her and took her by the hand, leading her to the large play mat. The contact supervisor was typing and Lily was sitting on the sofa.

'Come and join us,' I said to Lily.

Reluctantly, she stood, came over and sat heavily on the mat. Her face was expressionless. There was a large basket of toy cars, people, animals and so forth close by. I began taking them out and setting them on the mat. Olivia tipped the basket over and then began to play with the figures. Lily just sat there watching her.

'Let's play,' I said.

Lily picked up one of the people and set him down in the park by a pretend river and then continued to sit there. Olivia played with the figures, putting ducks on the river and a dog on a lead, which she gave to the man. I wondered again how you teach an adult to play. It certainly didn't come naturally, not to Lily at least. She sat there just watching Olivia, not making any move to join in. I had assumed it would be easier this week. Olivia stood and went over to the window. I guessed that, like in most contact centres, the children here could play outside on a nice day, but it was very cold and no one was out there today.

Olivia turned, and as she did so she spotted the giant card wedged behind the contact supervisor's desk. She began to tug on it.

'No! Don't do that,' Lily shouted. She jumped up and ran to stop her.

Olivia burst into tears and ran to me.

'Don't shout at her,' I told Lily. 'She's a child and doesn't understand.'

'Well, she shouldn't have touched it,' Lily said. 'It's for next week.'

I'd seen other parents react as Lily did and it isn't nice to watch. I dried Olivia's tears and sat her on my lap on the play mat.

'Let's do something else,' I suggested. She seemed to have lost interest in the play mat. 'What do you like to do?'

There was a small table with four chairs in one corner. Olivia pointed.

'Let's have some tea,' I said.

I lifted Olivia off my lap and we went over to the table, where I sat in one of the chairs. Olivia began playing with the kitchen set that was to hand. I looked over at Lily who was watching us.

'Come and play,' I encouraged her.

She slowly stood and, with no emotion, came over and sat at the small table. The contact supervisor was typing.

'That's a lovely cake,' I said to Olivia.

She had put a pink plastic iced cake on my plate. I pretended to take a bite. She put a yellow iced cake on Lily's plate. Lily sat there looking at it.

'Oh, and a fried egg,' I said as it landed on my plate. 'And a sausage. Aren't I lucky!'

Slowly my toy plate filled with food. Lily's was the same. Oliva began to laugh. It was a real chuckle. The last item she put on my plate was a slice of toast.

'Yummy,' I said and pretended to take a bite.

Olivia looked at it, then picked it up and tried to bite it.

'No, yucky,' I said, pulling a face. 'It's plastic.'

'Yucky,' Olivia said and pulled a similar face.

I laughed. We continued to play with the pretend food for some time. Children usually love this activity, copying the adults they have seen doing this at home. Then, as two-year-olds do, she lost interest and spotted a doll in bed. She went over and tucked her in. Then she turned to the pretend sink and began washing up.

Too soon it was the end of the session and we were advised to say goodbye to Olivia; the contact supervisor would then take her out. I knew that Lily's behaviour had been no better this week than last. Indeed, I thought it had been worse.

'Bye bye, love,' I said to Olivia.

'Bye,' Lily said.

The contact supervisor closed her laptop and picked up the present and card.

'I'll give it to Olivia's parents,' she told us.

She held Olivia's hand and I waved as Olivia left the room. She gave a little wave back. Lily had taken out her phone by now and was looking at it. I didn't say anything at that point. I signed us out and then waited until we were in the car.

'How do you feel it went?' I asked once I was driving.

'OK.'

I glanced at her and continued to drive.

'I don't,' I said pointedly.

Lily took her eyes from her phone. 'Don't what?'

'I don't think the session went very well at all. I think we can improve on it.'

'That's your opinion,' she said sombrely and returned to her phone.

'It is, Lily, and if you follow my example and play with Olivia, I think it would be a lot better for you both.'

'I can't do what you do. You've done it for years,' she said moodily.

'Can you try?' I asked. 'Try to copy me and play with Olivia.'

'She's fine,' Lily said dismissively.

I knew she wasn't 'fine'. I also knew that the contact supervisor had been writing about Lily's apparent lack of commitment. True, she'd bought Olivia a birthday present and a very large card, but any fool can wrap up a present and buy a card. She'd written *I love you so much* in the card, but Olivia needed to see that in her behaviour.

'I think you need to try to show Olivia you care,' I said.

She shrugged, and after a few moments she said, 'But I don't know how to.'

'Playing with her and enjoying your time with her is a good start. Children love to play; that's what they do all day. If you join in her games, she'll start to take notice of you. At present you could be anyone who's just come into the room and sat there.'

'I'll try,' she said too readily, and put her earphones in.

I didn't know what else to say; I'd done my best. I could only hope that next week would be a lot better, but I had my doubts. If Lily didn't improve her relationship with Olivia, I knew where this was going to lead.

Lily kept her earphones in listening to music during the drive home. There were no hold-ups this time and we got home just after Paula at 6.30 p.m. She was busy making dinner – pasta in a sauce with vegetables, which looked and smelt delicious. I could smell it in the hall.

Lily went straight to her room while I went into the kitchen.

'Hi, love,' I said, pleased to see her, and kissed her cheek.

'Mum, do you know where my earphones are?' she asked, stirring the pasta.

'No, aren't they in your bedroom?'

'No,' she said.

Then I had a thought. 'Have you lent them to Lily? She was wearing some today and I've never seen her use those earphones before.'

'No, I didn't. If they are mine, I didn't give permission,' Paula said. 'They were in my bedroom this morning. I always leave them there when I go to work.'

I also knew she always closed her bedroom door before she left. It was a habit we'd all got into.

'Let me check,' I said, and I went upstairs.

I knocked on Lily's bedroom door. There was no reply. I assumed she couldn't hear me because she was wearing the earphones, so I knocked again and slowly opened the door. She was facing away from me.

'Lily,' I said, touching her shoulder.

She jumped and removed an earpiece.

'Where did you get the earphones from?'

'Paula,' she said.

'From her bedroom?'

'Yes.'

'Did you ask her if you could borrow them?'

'No. What's the problem? I took them. She doesn't use them during the day. I knew she wouldn't mind.'

'No, but I'd like you to ask me or Paula in future. I'm sure she would have agreed, but you shouldn't have just gone into her bedroom and taken them. It's not something we do here.'

I assumed that when she was sleeping at friends' homes she had helped herself to whatever she needed.

'Will you take them off now, please?' I said. 'You can save up to buy yourself some from your pocket money.'

She pulled a face. I waited. There was a few seconds' pause before she yanked them off and shoved them towards me.

'Thank you,' I said. 'In future, please ask Paula. I know she won't mind.'

She didn't say anything further and I left the room holding the earphones; I didn't close Lily's bedroom door. As I went into Paula's room to leave the earphones I heard Lily's bedroom door slam hard. It seemed that she was simmering with anger the whole time and it didn't take much for it to come out. Paula was too nice to do what I'd just done and ask for their return, but they were expensive earphones and quite new. It was true we didn't just help ourselves to items from other people's bedrooms.

'I've put them in your bedroom,' I said to Paula. 'Lily borrowed them for the day.'

'But I left them in my room this morning.'

'I know, and I've told her she's not to go into your room again without asking.'

'Thanks, Mum.'

'How's Liam?' I asked.

'Good, thanks. We're seeing each other tomorrow.'

'Lovely.'

The pasta was ready and Lily joined us for dinner. Nothing more was said about the earphones.

'How did your visit go today?' Paula asked Lily, making conversation.

'OK.'

And that was all Lily said on the matter of the contact she'd waited two years for.

CHAPTER TWENTY-TWO

I HAVEN'T SLEPT AT NIGHT

The following Monday was Olivia's birthday and Lily told me as soon as she was up.

'I wonder if she's opened my present yet?' she said, coming downstairs and looking vaguely happy.

'I don't know, but I'm sure she'll love it.'

Lily wondered about Olivia and what she was doing for most of the day. I think she thought someone would phone and thank her for the present, but of course that wasn't going to happen. It was the following morning when we got a call from Eva. First, she spoke to me. Lily was in her bedroom.

'Cathy, how are you?' she asked.

'Fine, thank you, and you?'

'Good.' She paused, then said, 'I hope you won't take this the wrong way. I appreciate all you're doing for Lily, but I'd prefer it if you didn't go into contact with her any more. Could you wait outside in your car?'

'I could. Why? What's the problem?' I asked.

'I think you've become too involved with Olivia. She seems to be bonding with you rather than having anything to do with Lily. Lily is going to have to work a lot harder to get her love and attention.' I assumed this had come from the contact supervisor.

'If I'm honest, it had crossed my mind that I was getting too close,' I said. 'But what else could I do? Lily is struggling to play with Olivia.'

'I know that's an issue. I'll speak to Lily now if I may.'

'Yes, of course.'

I took the phone upstairs to Lily and told her that it was Eva. I returned downstairs and went into the kitchen. I could hear Lily's raised voice but not what she was saying. A few minutes later she came thundering downstairs, the phone still in her hand.

'She wants to speak to you again,' she said, and thrust the phone at me.

I frowned, puzzled, as I took it.

'Sorry,' Eva said, sounding flustered. 'I've upset Lily badly. Please phone me if she doesn't calm down. I've got to go out of the office now. I've told her that contact will go ahead on Thursday at 2 p.m. and you will wait outside. I tried to explain why, but she's not happy with me.'

'All right,' I said, and the call ended.

'She's a rotten old bag,' Lily fumed. 'She wants me to fail, I know she does. She's told me I have to go into contact alone in future.'

'Yes, I know. She's just told me that, but it's not a problem.'

'I'm not going in if you can't come,' she yelled, glaring at me.

'Lily, calm down, please, and think about it. It's very unusual for someone other than close family to be allowed into contact at all.'

'I don't care!' she shouted. 'I want you there!' And, turning, she stomped off upstairs.

I left her to it. This was Lily and I knew she would calm down. Over the course of the morning, she slowly returned to normal. She asked me for her pocket money early. I had been giving it to her at the weekend but this week she wanted to buy some earphones, so I gave her the ten pounds from the following weekend and she went straight out and bought them from a shop in the High Street. She came back in a good mood and didn't take them off again at all, effectively blocking out the world. She even ate dinner with them in. I didn't say anything. Parental control is about knowing what to try to change, and it didn't really matter, although it's true that I would never have allowed one of my children to eat dinner wearing earphones.

On Thursday morning I prepared to drive Lily to Newcastle. It was assumed I would still take her. Lily hadn't spoken about Olivia or contact since the phone call from Eva, and I hadn't brought it up either. I packed sandwiches and drinks and told Paula to expect us when she saw us and we kissed goodbye. I pressed the sat nav for the contact centre and put the radio on as Lily was wearing her earphones.

The drive was the same as last time and we arrived at the contact centre at 1 p.m. We ate our sandwiches – Lily still with her earphones in. Once she'd finished eating, I tapped her on the shoulder and asked her to take them off as I wanted to talk to her, which she did.

'How are you feeling?' I said.

'Not good,' she admitted. 'I don't think I can go through with it.'

'Why not?' I asked. I'd had the feeling she was low.

'I don't know. I guess it's because Olivia seems to be in charge.'

'But that's how two-year-olds behave,' I said. 'They haven't learnt to be fearful of the world, that's why they need protecting.'

She shrugged and looked through her side window.

'Is there anything specific you want to talk about?' I asked.

I accepted that I had years and years of childcare experience, but Lily, as far as I knew, had none. If she was ever going to be allowed to parent Olivia, I knew it was going to be a long, painful process.

'Not really. Olivia is just a very confident child.'

'I think that if you take the lead, she will follow you,' I suggested. 'When you get inside the contact room why not take some toys from the shelves and start playing with them? Or sit at the small table by the kitchen. She likes playing with that.'

'I'll try,' she said, and put her earpieces back in. I assumed they gave her a sense of protection from all that she couldn't cope with. I left her alone.

A little before 2 p.m. we saw Holly and James's car draw up, but only Holly got out. James wasn't there this time. Holly took Olivia out of the back of the car and they walked into the contact centre. Lily watched them go in but didn't say anything. At 2 p.m. I suggested to Lily that she put away her earphones and go in. She silently took them out and left them with her phone on the seat.

'Good luck,' I said.

She didn't reply.

I watched her go to the main gate, press the bell and then wait to be admitted.

Once she was inside, I got out of the car and went for a walk. I'd be back in plenty of time, but I find walking helps clear my head. It was very cold, with a biting easterly wind. I walked around the surrounding streets but after about half an hour I headed back to the car. It was too cold. As I turned the corner I saw Holly by her car talking on her phone. I didn't know if she knew me or not, but I was the only one waiting in the car park. She looked over, saw me and suddenly ran over.

'Are you Cathy Glass?' she asked.

'Yes.'

'Is Lily Saunders staying with you?'

'She is.'

She was well spoken and wearing a cream coat with matching boots and hat.

'Would you please tell Lily to leave us alone,' she said, tears immediately forming in her eyes. 'We were going to adopt Olivia, but that's all been put on hold now. I don't know what's happening any more. Please tell her.' Her tears were flowing freely now.

'I'm sorry for your upset,' I said. 'But I can't tell Lily to leave you alone. Olivia is her daughter, after all.'

'No, she's not her daughter. She hasn't seen her since she had her in hospital. The system in this country is appalling. It's failing. We've had to keep looking after Olivia, not knowing if we can keep her or not. Olivia is so confused and so am I. James couldn't face coming here today.'

'I'm so sorry,' I said again. 'But there is nothing I can do.'

'You must be able to talk to Lily,' she said. 'Before it's too late. You're a foster carer. Lily doesn't want Olivia. I don't know how much of this I can take. I haven't slept at night since we were told. James says we should pull out of the adoption altogether.'

'But you're her parents. Olivia calls you Mummy and Daddy,' I said.

'I know, but we might not be in the future,' she said and, turning, ran back to her car and got in.

I returned to my own car and stared through the windscreen at the blue BMW where Holly was sitting, very upset. It wouldn't have been appropriate for me to go over and try to talk to her, not the foster carer of the mother of the child she was hoping to adopt. I wouldn't have known what to say either, so I stayed where I was, watching. I could only guess at her distress. However, what I didn't like was the fact that her husband was having doubts about continuing with the adoption. I hoped he didn't mean it and had only said it during an upset. This was the big problem with fostering for adoption, also known as early permanence: while it offers the child stability, it is the exact opposite for the hopeful parents-to-be. The natural parents can change their mind at any point before the case goes to court, so the children are carefully selected by the social services for that reason. Just as Olivia had been. Who would have thought that Lily would change her mind after nearly two years? Though that wasn't to say the judge would send Olivia to live with her mother. Ultimately, it would be the judge's decision.

At 2.45, a quarter of an hour before the contact was due to end, Lily came out of the building and walked quickly to my car. Holly was still in hers and I hoped she wouldn't approach Lily. I could see there would be an argument if she did. Holly stayed in her car, although she must have seen Lily pass. Lily came straight to me and got in. Holly immediately left her car and went into the contact centre.

'Is everything OK?' I asked.

'Olivia was upset,' was all she said, and she put her earpieces in.

I didn't start the car. I tapped her on the shoulder.

'What?' she said curtly, removing an earpiece.

'Take them off,' I said. 'I want to talk to you. Why was Olivia upset?'

'I don't know. She kept wanting her mummy.'

She put her earpieces back in. Holly hadn't appeared from the contact centre yet. I started the car and slowly drove away. I had a lot on my mind, thinking about Olivia and what Holly had said. After about half an hour I tapped Lily's shoulder again.

'What is it?' she asked.

'Take your earpieces out,' I said brusquely. 'I need to talk to you.' I waited while she did as I'd asked. 'Are you serious about wanting to parent Olivia? I mean really serious.'

'Of course.'

'Only I think you are causing Holly and James a lot of upset.'

'How do you know that?'

'While I was waiting for you, Holly came over and spoke to me. She was really upset.'

'That's her problem,' she said with attitude.

'But it's been created by you, Lily. In a few months Olivia would have been theirs.'

'What are you saying? That I shouldn't apply to have Olivia because Holly and James want her?'

'No, but I think it needs a lot of thought. This is going to be forever and you're very young.'

'I was old enough to have a baby,' she snapped back.

'True. But I want you to give the whole thing some more thought, now you've spent some time with Olivia. Put yourself in the place of a parent. Olivia would be with you the whole time, twenty-four-seven.'

'Until she goes to nursery,' Lily said. 'Then I can get my life back.' She'd obviously given it some thought, although not in a particularly healthy way. 'Is that everything?' she asked.

'What happened in contact?'

'I told you. Olivia was upset. That's it.'

She put her earpieces back in and left me to worry about Olivia and her parents. I hoped that James wasn't having second thoughts about adopting.

It was the following Tuesday when Eva called Lily's mobile and told her that Olivia was no longer with Holly and James, but had been moved to live with other foster carers. When Lily told me the news I was absolutely horrified. Olivia had been with them since birth. 'That poor child,' I said.

'Does that mean that it will be easier for me to get her back?' Lily asked.

I looked at her. 'I have no idea.'

CHAPTER TWENTY-THREE

VERY WORRIED

Lily said that contact was going ahead at the centre as usual at 2 p.m. on Thursday. Eva hadn't asked to speak to me when she told Lily the news about Olivia – she didn't have to – but I was devastated. Holly and James must have told Eva that they didn't want to adopt Olivia any more after Lily had reappeared. I could imagine their heartbreak in coming to that decision. Olivia had been their baby right from the start. They loved her, of that there was no doubt. If they'd just waited, the matter would have gone to court and then, through their barrister, they could have made a good case for keeping Olivia with them permanently. Clearly, they didn't want a fight. I can't say what the judge's decision would have been, but if I'd had to guess, I would have said that Olivia would likely have stayed with them. Clearly they couldn't wait to find out. I knew there would be no second chance. I'd never heard of a child being returned to the prospective adopters once they'd given them up.

I was really sad all day. I just kept thinking about Olivia going to a new foster home. It would be the start of a very unsettled period that would follow her into adulthood, I was certain. In later life, she wouldn't remember what had happened to her at the age of two, but I could picture her disquiet. Lily, on the other hand, seemed quite chirpy at the news. I could guess why. When she'd changed her mind and decided she wanted to parent Olivia, she'd been presented with her in a ready-made loving family, which was difficult for Lily to adjust to. Now that Olivia was with new foster carers, she'd be floundering. I wondered what she would do when she saw Lily. Be very confused and upset, I thought.

On Wednesday Eva phoned me and asked if I was aware of the news about Olivia.

'Yes,' I said. 'And I'm very disturbed. How is she doing?'

'She was moved to Angela and Peter Miller's late on Monday and she's slowly settling in.' Which meant nothing in my book. 'I shall be at the contact centre on Thursday for a least some of the session,' Eva continued. 'I was wondering if you could go to contact at the start of the session. I think it might help Olivia.' I noticed she hadn't mention Lily.

'Yes, of course.'

'Thank you. As you can imagine, this wasn't a decision that Holly and James came to lightly.'

'I appreciate that.'

'I tried to dissuade them, but they'd made up their minds. They're convinced that Olivia will be given to Lily, but that's not what my report said.'

'Did you tell them that?' I asked

'Yes, but it didn't do any good. They'd decided, I'm afraid.' She sighed. 'So here we are. I'll see you on

Thursday. I'll stay for about half an hour. Can you tell Lily, please?'

'Yes, of course.'

As soon as the call ended I went upstairs and told Lily that Eva had just phoned me and asked that I stay at the contact session for a while, and that Eva would be there too.

'Why?' she asked.

'Eva asked me to be there, and the social worker can attend whenever she likes.'

'Really? I didn't know that,' Lily said, and put her earpieces back in.

Thankfully we hadn't had any more snow and no more was forecast. On Thursday morning I said goodbye to Paula and, as before, told her to expect us when she saw us. With our sandwiches and drinks in a bag, I drove to the motorway and stopped – there'd been an accident about a mile further up. We were held up there for nearly an hour, during which time Lily became increasingly agitated.

'We'll be late or I'll miss contact completely,' she said repeatedly.

I began to get ruffled too. Eventually the traffic began to move forward, and we pulled into the car park a few minutes before 2 p.m.

I parked and we sprang out and went into the centre, where I gave our names to the receptionist. It was a different receptionist to the last three times. She told us which room to go to – a different one – and we signed in. Lily seemed to be taking it all in her stride now she knew we weren't late. The door to the room was closed so I knocked, and we heard Eva call, 'Come in.' Lily went in first. It was a smaller room than the others, and inside sat the contact supervisor, Eva, another woman and Olivia, who had hold of Eva's skirt and was hanging on to it tightly.

'This is Angela Miller,' Eva said, introducing the other woman. 'The new foster carer.'

'Oh, hello,' I said. 'I'm Cathy.'

'Eva has been telling me all about you. Olivia came to us on Monday afternoon, so she's still getting to know us all.'

'How has she been?' I asked, looking at Olivia, who was clinging on to Eva's skirt for all she was worth.

'She's pretty upset, as you can imagine,' Angela replied. 'But the previous carers have sent all her belongings, including clothes and toys, so that's good. Anyway, I'd better be off now. I know you want to start. I'll be waiting in the car park. It's not worth me driving home.'

'OK,' I said. 'I'm staying in here for a while. Nice to meet you.'

'And you.'

Angela said goodbye to Olivia, but she was still holding on to Eva's skirt. The poor child was clinging to the only person she knew. Eva would have been visiting her since she was born. Lily was standing by me, not sure what to do. She looked completely thrown.

'Hello, love,' I said gently, going down to Olivia's level.

She withdrew even more. Eva picked her up and sat her on the sofa next to her.

'Let's have a look at this book,' she said, and picked up a book that had been left on the sofa.

She opened it and began to read. But Olivia was looking at Lily and me a little way from her.

'Let's sit down,' I said to Lily.

We moved a couple of children's chairs closer to the sofa and sat. Eva had her arm around Olivia as she read the story. Gradually, Olivia's gaze went from us to the book. She sat there silently and appeared to be listening. When Eva finished she stood, ready to return the book. Olivia frantically grabbed her skirt and hung on to her. Eva took her hand and guided her to the bookshelf.

'You choose another story,' she said gently, and put the book back on the shelf.

Olivia did nothing. Eva began looking through the assortment of books. They were for all ages of children. Oliva must have spotted the one she wanted and pointed. Eva took it down. It was the book I'd read about animals. Who said that a child of two can't remember?

Olivia hung on to Eva's skirt again as she returned to the sofa.

'Lily, do you want to read it to Olivia?' Eva asked.

Lily shrugged. 'Don't mind.'

But Olivia clearly wanted Eva to read her the book and continued to cling to her. Eva opened the book at the first page about the frog and read it. Olivia looked at me, not understanding, or possibly wanting me to read it. When Eva had finished the book she said to Olivia, 'Would you like to do something with Lily now?'

She shrank back into Eva.

Of the adults in the room Lily was the least appealing, I thought, sitting there with a sullen expression on her face and not doing anything.

I got up and fetched some of the items from the toy kitchen similar to the ones she'd played with before. There weren't so many to choose from in this room. I brought them over and sat down. I pretended I was making lunch – a fried egg, sausage, tomato, etcetera. I fried them in a frying pan and gave the sausage to Lily on a small plate. Then I gave a fried egg to Olivia. She sat there with it, staring at me and doing nothing.

'Yummy,' I said, pretending to eat the tomato I had on my plate.

Olivia continued to sit there, very close to Eva, her world turned upside down. It was an indication of the level of her trauma that she couldn't even play with anything today. All she seemed to want to do was cuddle Eva. I tried a variety of toys, which I took from around the room, but nothing interested her. Half an hour passed and Eva said, 'Cathy, do you want to go out for a while? Lily can stay with Olivia and me.'

'Yes, OK.' I knew she would be safe with Eva there.

I stood and said goodbye to Olivia. She looked at me with huge eyes and again hung on tightly to Eva's skirt.

As I left I breathed a deep sigh and made my way to the exit. I signed out and left the centre, deeply troubled. I began to think of all sorts of scenarios. I knew I couldn't offer to adopt Olivia as I would be considered too old. The social services would want someone in their late twenties to late thirties. Adrian and Kirsty? But they'd only just begun to be assessed. As I was on the way to my car, Angela got out of her car.

'Hi, Cathy,' she called, and came over. 'How's Olivia doing?'

'Not very well,' I said. 'She's just sitting there.'

'It's only the first contact since the move,' she said. 'Eva told me that Lily wants her back.'

'That's what she's saying.'

'But you don't think she's going to get her?'

'I honestly don't know.'

'It's strange the way the social services work. We have two older boys that we have on Special Guardianship Orders, but we're not allowed to adopt them.'

A Special Guardianship Order (SGO) is a court order that provides a long-term placement for a child who cannot live with their parents. It differs from adoption, as it doesn't end the legal relationship between the child and their birth parents, but if anyone wants to remove the child they need to go to court.

'I guess the boys are older then?' I asked, not really concentrating on her reply.

'Yes, eight and ten. They're not related. We can have up to four children in our house. My husband is a full-time carer too.'

'Will you be getting another child?' I asked, thinking of Olivia.

'It depends on the social services.'

I knew that some foster-carer couples both fostered full-time. But my thoughts were with little Olivia, who now had two older brothers to contend with.

'How is Olivia doing at home?' I asked Angela.

'We were up most of Monday and Tuesday night, as you can imagine. Last night she was so exhausted she slept. She'll get over it in time. She'll have to.' She gave a little laugh. 'They always do.'

'How many children have you fostered?' I asked.

'Olivia is our eighty-ninth. We've been doing it for fifteen years.'

'That's good,' I said. 'Will you offer Olivia permanency if she can't go back to Lily?'

'Oh, no. Two boys are plenty for us. She'll be found another adoptive home. She's a sweet kid.'

Another move, I thought, making Olivia even more distrustful of people.

Angela's mobile sounded. 'Sorry, I've got to take this,' she said, and moved away.

I went back to my car and finished the packet of juice I'd brought with us. Ten minutes later Angela came over.

'Guess what? We've got another one coming now. A boy, aged seven. That's all we know about him. My husband will be at home to receive him if I'm not back in time. It's all go here.'

I could see that Angela really liked her job.

Three o'clock was fast approaching and we decided it was time to go back into the centre and collect Olivia and Lily. Angela pressed the bell and we were admitted.

'Go down to the room,' the receptionist told us.

Olivia was as I'd left her, snuggled close to Eva on the sofa. I looked around for Lily, but there was no sign of her.

'Where's Lily?' I asked Eva.

'She said she was going to the toilet but that was over fifteen minutes ago,' Eva said.

'I'd better go and check on her,' I said. 'Perhaps she's ill.'

'I hope she's all right,' Angela called after me.

I went first to the bathroom that was at the end of the corridor and checked the three cubicles. She wasn't in there. She couldn't have left by the front door; I would have seen her. I went back down the corridor and turned left. I passed the kitchen and looked in. Then I spotted her, opening and closing cupboard doors in the kitchen.

'What are you doing in here?' I asked, going in.

'I wanted a hot chocolate, but they don't seem to have any.'

'Is it for Olivia?' I asked.

'No, for me.'

I couldn't believe it. She'd left an hour's contact over fifteen minutes early to make herself a hot chocolate. Didn't she understand the importance of contact?

'Come on,' I said firmly. 'You need to say goodbye to Olivia. It's three o'clock now.'

She closed the cupboard she was searching and came back with me. Eva was just getting Olivia into her coat.

'Oh, there you are,' Eva said to Lily. 'I thought we'd lost you.'

'Why's it such a big deal?' Lily said, aggrieved. 'I was going to make a hot chocolate.'

'It's the end of the session,' Eva said. 'Are you going to say goodbye to Olivia?'

'Bye,' Lily said, and threw her a small wave.

'Bye, love,' I said. She had her coat on now.

'I'll walk her to your car,' Eva said to Angela, and we all left the room together.

As Eva helped Olivia into the back of Angela's car she began to cry. 'Mummy, Mummy,' she said over and over again.

My own eyes filled.

I knew there was nothing I could do, so I left Eva talking calmly to Olivia and said goodbye to Angela.

'I'll see you next week,' she said.

Lily was standing by my car waiting for me to open the door. We got in and I pressed home on the sat nav. As I drove past Angela's car I could see Eva leaning in and gently talking to Olivia.

'Lily,' I said before she had a chance to put her earphones in. 'What is your understanding of contact?'

'It's when a parent sees their child.'

'That's right. It's a showcase for how well they can parent their child. What made you leave contact a quarter of an hour early to make yourself a hot chocolate? I don't understand.'

'I needed the toilet.'

'Then you should have gone straight back into the room after you'd used it, not looked for a hot chocolate.'

'So?' she said sullenly.

'It will not have gone unnoticed.'

'Well, I didn't know, did I?' Lily snapped.

Perhaps I was expecting too much of Lily. She was only eighteen, after all. Yet part of me said she should have instinctively wanted to stay with Olivia for the full hour – and longer – like other parents visiting their children on contact did. I'd seen this time and time again: the parents were in tears when they had to leave, but not Lily.

CHAPTER TWENTY-FOUR

STAYING WITH FRIENDS

The following day the literature arrived from the college. I had a look through and gave it to Lily.

'I've marked the pages I think are appropriate,' I said to her.

We were still waiting for legal aid to come through. We hadn't heard any more since Mr Stanley had sent that first letter going over what we'd discussed when we'd seen him.

On Saturday morning Lucy arrived with her two children, Emma and Theo. It was partly to return the sledge she'd borrowed for nursery, but she stayed for nearly two hours. I made coffee and a snack and played with her children – they were growing so quickly. Paula and then Lily also came downstairs and talked to her.

'How is Lily getting on with her daughter?' Lucy asked me in the kitchen. 'She never talks about her, and when I asked her about it she just said it was going "OK".'

'I know, it's strange. I don't know how sincere she is in wanting to be Olivia's parent. She says she does, but her actions don't really show it. My worry is that Olivia will be given to Lily, then she'll feel she's had enough and can't cope any more. It would be devastating for the child to have to leave another home.'

'She wouldn't do that, would she?'

'I honestly don't know.'

On Sunday Adrian, Kirsty and Sophia paid us an impromptu visit. I feel very blessed that my children live so close and can pop in when they please. I cut up a cake I'd bought the day before. Lily didn't come down but Paula did. I took Lily up a slice of cake before it all vanished.

'How is Lily?' Kirsty asked on my return downstairs.

'I think she's all right,' I said.

'And what about her daughter?'

'She's a really sweet kid. I don't know if Lily will get her back. We're waiting for the legal aid to come through.'

We talked a bit about fostering and I played with Sophia as I spoke. Adrian was talking to Paula. The afternoon vanished and then they left and the house was quiet again. It was five o'clock when Paula said, 'Liam and I are going to the cinema tonight. He's coming here to collect me at six-thirty, so you can meet him.'

'Wonderful.'

As it turned out I was only allowed to say a quick hello and goodbye at the door, but from what I saw of him he seemed very nice.

On Monday, Eva called Lily's mobile. It was mid-morning and once they'd finished Lily came downstairs and said that contact was going to be increased to twice a week. Tuesdays and Thursdays.

'That's excellent,' I said. I was pleased. It was a positive sign.

'Eva said you can come in for a quarter of an hour to begin with but that's all.'

'OK.'

'But supposing I want you there for longer?' Lily asked.

'If you get Olivia back, I won't be there at all.'

'It'll be different then. I'll know what I'm doing. I've just told Eva that I want you there for as long as I feel I need you, otherwise there will just be me and the contact supervisor.'

Sometimes Lily was so vulnerable and needy; I felt for her deeply.

'All right,' I said. 'If she's agreed.'

So on Tuesday we both got into my car and I drove us to Newcastle. Eva had timed the contact at 2 p.m. again to give us a chance to get there. It would be for an hour as before, and I'd put sandwiches and drinks in a bag and told Paula to expect us home whenever we arrived.

'It's a lot of driving for you,' Paula said.

'I know, love. But it won't be forever.'

Once again, Lily had her earphones in the whole way, so I put the radio on. I felt we could have used this time to get to know each other better, but I'd tried to make conversation and had been thwarted by a single word or a bullet line. I reminded myself that Lily was young.

We arrived at the centre without any hold-ups, and ate our sandwiches, Lily still with her earpieces in. At 2 p.m. she took them out and we got out of the car and headed towards the contact centre. As we walked by a large black six-seater car on our right, the driver's door opened and a man got out.

'Hi, you must be Cathy. I'm Peter Miller,' he said.

I realized he would be Angela's husband, and as he spoke I glanced into the back of the car and saw Olivia in a child's seat.

'Hello,' I said, and smiled and waved at Olivia.

Peter came round and opened the door to help Olivia out of the car.

'Angela is looking after our seven-year-old who arrived last week,' he said. 'He's a handful! I'll see Olivia in, then I need to be off. How long is this contact for?'

'An hour,' I said.

He raised his eyes and took hold of Olivia's hand.

'This is Lily, Olivia's mother,' I said, introducing her.

'Hi,' he said.

We went in and the receptionist recognized us.

'Sign in, please. You're in the same room as last time. Straight down the corridor.'

Lily was standing by my side, making no attempt to speak to or interact with Olivia. We finished signing in and went along the corridor and into the room the receptionist had directed us to. The contact supervisor was already sitting at her desk. She looked up and smiled as we entered. 'Come in,' she said.

'Bye, Olivia,' Peter said as soon as we entered. 'See you later.'

He turned and left her, closing the door behind him. Olivia just stood there looking lost and alone.

'Go over and say hi,' I said quietly to Lily.

Olivia looked at Lily and Lily looked back. Then Olivia began to cry. I instinctively went to her.

'Why is she crying?' Lily asked. 'We've only just arrived.'

'Because she's had a lot of change in her life recently and doesn't know anyone. Let's make her feel better,' I said.

I took her by the hand as Lily wasn't doing anything and led her to the sofa. I wondered what Lily would have done if I hadn't been there.

'Come on, love,' I said to Olivia. 'You're going to be all right.'

'Mummy, Mummy,' she said. Then, 'Eva.'

'Eva's not here today, but I'm sure you'll see her again. Let's play with something.'

I thought Olivia would have some recollection of our previous session last Thursday. Certainly, she'd remember today on Thursday.

I dried her eyes and got out the book on animals that seemed to have become her favourite. I read it, making the noises – *ribbit, ribbit, oink, oink, neigh, neigh,* and so forth. She wanted me to read it again, which I did. Then I said, 'Lily read it now,' and passed the book to her. She was sitting on the sofa on the other side of Olivia.

She began to read but Olivia got up and went to the toy kitchen.

'She doesn't want me to read the book,' Lily said, disgruntled.

'She might do later,' I said. 'Let's play in the kitchen.'

After about another quarter of an hour of playing I stood to leave.

'Where are you going?' Lily asked.

'To wait outside the door.'

I began towards it. Olivia ran after me and grabbed the leg of my trousers. I led her back into the room towards Lily.

'She wants you to stay,' Lily said. 'So do I.'

I sat down. I tried to leave again after about another ten minutes, but Oliva ran after me again. Lily did nothing to help her stay at all. At that point I gave up.

'Shall I read her the book?' Lily asked, referring to the one about animals.

'You can try, but I'm not sure she wants it read now,' I said.

Lily took the book to her, but Olivia turned away.

By the end of the session, I thought Lily was no better at relating to her daughter than she had been four weeks ago. I hadn't been able to leave contact as Eva had suggested. I thought that the only way was for me not to go into the contact at all.

At 3 p.m. there was a sharp tap on the door and Peter came in. 'Come on, it's time to go,' he said to Olivia.

He took her hand and coat and they left in a hurry. By the time Lily and I were in the car park their car had gone.

'I'm going to do as Eva originally said and not come in on Thursday,' I said as we walked to my car. 'My being there isn't doing you any good. If there is just you and Olivia, she won't have anyone else to relate to.'

Lily didn't like my suggestion at all.

'That's not fair!' she said loudly. 'Supposing I need you?'

'I'll just be outside the door.'

On Wednesday morning Lily received two letters addressed to her. She opened them: one was advising her that she had qualified for legal aid and the other was from universal credit saying her month's money would be deposited into her bank account within the next few days. She was delighted and eagerly checked her bank account, but it hadn't arrived yet.

'At least you have legal aid,' I said.

'Now I can properly fight for Olivia,' she replied.

I wasn't sure what she thought was going to happen with legal aid; most of the proof of whether she could parent Olivia would be on her performance at contact. At present I thought we were a long way from satisfying that criteria, but I could be wrong.

On Thursday morning her universal credit was in her bank account. She ran downstairs, elated, to tell me.

'Remember, it has to last you the month,' I warned her.

'Yes, I know.'

We went to Newcastle as usual on that day. Lily spent a lot of the journey texting. I had the radio on. We arrived in plenty of time, had our sandwiches and then I saw Peter going in. He was in a hurry again, and I wasn't surprised, with three boys to look after, one of them new in their house. I saw Lily into the contact room, then, as I'd said I would, I went outside to the waiting room. Most contact centres have a waiting room for relatives and foster carers to relax in during contact. Having told Lily where I was going, I went in, picked up a magazine and sat down. I began reading an article about the healing power of a tree!

A quarter of an hour later Lily came to find me, looking very worried.

'Olivia wants you,' she said. 'She keeps pointing to the door. I've run out of things to play with.'

She was in a room brimming with games and pastimes for all ages of children and she'd run out of things to play with? I didn't think so.

'What have you played with so far?' I asked, standing and returning to the room.

'Everything,' she said.

As we went into the room Olivia saw me and her eyes lit up.

Lily showed me some of the games she'd got out, like Connect 4 and Spirograph, which Olivia certainly couldn't do at her age.

'I used to like these,' she said.

Olivia was on her way to the bookshelf. She took out the book on animals and ran over to me with it.

I smiled. 'Let's read it,' I said to her.

'I've tried to read it to her,' Lily said, 'but she won't listen to me.'

'Let's both give it a try.'

I placed the book open between us and read a few lines, then I suggested to Lily that she read it. Olivia knew her mind and immediately returned it to the shelf.

'There! I told you,' Lily snapped.

'So, find something else to do. You've only got half an hour left.'

'What?' she asked, looking around.

I glanced at the contact supervisor, who was looking at us.

Olivia had now gone to the home corner and was busy undressing a doll ready for bed. I guessed she felt safe in that space.

'Go over and join her,' I told Lily.

She stood and reluctantly went over and sat on one of the small children's chairs and watched Olivia play.

After about ten minutes I slipped out of the room again and stood on the other side of the door. I could see

Lily through the glass. She was sitting there expressionless, just watching Olivia play. As I looked, I saw her take out her phone and text someone. The contact supervisor saw it too. Her phone must have been on silent, but instead of ignoring it she'd answered it. In the end she kept checking and texting for about five minutes while Olivia played. It was only an hour's contact and unless it was considered an emergency it was ill advised to use your phone during that time.

At 3 p.m. Peter came up the corridor behind me.

'Time to go in,' he said.

We went into the room and Peter took Olivia out quite quickly, calling goodbye as he left. Lily was on her phone again.

'Bye,' I said to the contact supervisor.

'Goodbye.'

We signed out and once we were in the car park Lily said, 'Can you drop me off in Newcastle town? I'm going to stay up here for the weekend, then I'll see you at contact on Tuesday.'

This came as a bit of a shock, and I now realized what all the texting was about.

'Is that wise?' I asked. 'You haven't got any of your belongings with you.'

'I'll be fine.'

'Where will you stay?' I asked.

'With a friend.'

I knew she'd sofa-surfed when she'd been living here before.

'There's a party on Saturday,' she added.

What could I do? She was eighteen, but it also crossed my mind that the timing of this wasn't a coincidence. She now had over £300 from universal credit sitting in her bank account. I tried to dissuade her, but it was no good so ten minutes later I dropped her off outside Tyne and Wear Metro, where she was going to meet 'a friend'.

'I'll see you at contact on Tuesday,' I said. 'Have a nice time.'

But she was already speaking on her phone, so I drove away. I worried about her all the way home, as you do with teenagers. When I got in Paula was surprised to see me alone.

'Where's Lily?' she asked. 'I've made dinner.'

'She's staying with a friend in Newcastle. There was nothing I could do to dissuade her.'

'Is that wise?' Paula asked, as I had done. I knew she feared that it could lead Lily into trouble and away from her daughter again.

CHAPTER TWENTY-FIVE

NIGHTMARE

Late on Friday morning my mobile rang. It was Eva.

'Hello, Cathy, how are you?'

'Good, and you?'

'I can't complain. I wanted to ask you how contact has been, then I'll speak to Lily.'

'She's not here, I'm afraid,' I said. 'She wanted to stay with a friend in Newcastle for the weekend. I dropped her off outside the Tyne and Wear Metro after yesterday's contact.'

'Oh, I see. I wasn't aware of that.' There was a pause. 'I'm not happy with that. She's in a very stable environment with you.'

'I tried to dissuade her,' I said, 'but she was adamant. She said she'd see me again on Tuesday at contact.'

'I'll give her a ring shortly. How do you think contact is going?'

'It's early days yet,' I said diplomatically. 'I think Lily has a lot to learn. I think she cares for Olivia, but it has been difficult.'

'I placed Olivia with Angela and Peter as they were the only carers available. It's not ideal for Olivia to have three older boys in the house.' Eva would have been notified of the arrival of the third boy. 'So you think contact is going as well as can be expected?'

'Yes ... I guess that's a good way of putting it,' I said.

'Thank you for all you're doing. The contact supervisor has mentioned you in her report. I'll phone Lily now.'

I put the phone back into my pocket and continued with what I'd been doing – I was partway through cleaning the house. I was on the landing and about to go into Lily's room. I knew it was going to be a mess; she'd hardly left the room, only to go to contact. It was very difficult to get her out of the room for long enough to clean it. I went in and my expectations were immediately fulfilled. The bed was unmade, and the rest of the room was an absolute tip. I stripped the bed and put the sheets in the wash, opened the window for some fresh air, then turned the mattress and put on fresh sheets. Everyone likes fresh sheets.

As I was working I wondered what Lily was doing now, and decided it was none of my business. I continued tidying her room. Her new clothes were stuffed in the bottom of her wardrobe, not on hangers, so I hung them up. Her shoes were on the floor and the rubbish bin was overflowing. So that's where my Christmas box of Milk Tray had gone, I thought as I took it out. It was just as well Adrian couldn't see it. Aware of how much I liked Milk Tray, he'd bought me the box for Christmas. I think I'd had one chocolate.

I dusted the room and then hoovered. When I finished it looked a lot brighter. I closed the window and took the rubbish out, drawing the door to behind me. Whether Lily appreciated it or even noticed remained to be seen.

There's a different atmosphere in the house of a foster carer when a child is absent. It's as though something, or rather someone, is missing. Lily wasn't the easiest young person I'd looked after, but she was still quite young, I reminded myself. I had hopes for her and was looking forward to her returning on Tuesday.

Paula saw Liam on Friday and Saturday evening. They went out in a group on Friday and just the two of them on Saturday. She's always been very open and forthright in what she tells me. We had a relaxing day on Sunday. By Monday I was looking forward to seeing Lily again the following day, as I hoped she was me. I'd been tempted to phone her a number of times over the weekend, but I didn't until Tuesday morning. As I was getting into the car I phoned her mobile, but it went through to voicemail. It was a bit early for Lily to be up yet, I thought. I left a message saying, 'It's Cathy. I'll see you later. I'm just getting in my car to drive to contact. Bye, love.'

I'll admit, it was strange driving up to Newcastle alone, but I had the radio on BBC Radio 4; among other things, I listened to *Woman's Hour*. I arrived at the contact centre at 1 p.m. I switched off the engine and got out, stretched my legs, then returned to the car to eat my sandwiches. At 1.30 I phoned Lily again. I thought she might want a lift to the centre. No buses came along this road. My call went through to her voicemail again, which I thought was slightly odd.

'Lily, it's Cathy,' I said. 'Phone me if you need a lift to the contact centre. I'm here now.'

As I sat there looking through the windscreen I kept an eye on the path to the entrance to the contact centre, but Lily didn't appear.

At 1.55 Peter drew up in his black six-seater car. I got out and looked along the road for Lily before phoning her again. It went through to voicemail. 'It's Cathy. Where are you? We've got to go into the centre soon.'

'I don't think Lily is here yet,' I said to Peter, going over to him. 'She didn't stay the weekend with me.'

'Let's see if she's inside,' he said.

I knew Lily wasn't inside, unless she'd arrived over an hour early, which, given her timekeeping, wasn't likely.

We went into the contact centre and I asked if Lily Saunders had arrived.

'No, not yet,' the receptionist said.

Peter glanced at his watch. 'It's 2 p.m. I think the advice is that we wait twenty minutes and then leave.' This is to stop children becoming very disappointed if their parents don't arrive.

'Do you want to wait in the waiting room?' the receptionist asked us. 'I'll let you know when Lily arrives. She hasn't contacted us yet.' If a parent contacts the centre to say they are going to be late for contact, the centre keeps the contact open, as long as it doesn't become a regular occurrence.

Peter, Olivia and I went into the waiting room where there was a small box of children's toys. Peter took off Oliva's coat and hat. It was warm in there, so I unbuttoned mine too. Olivia silently began to take out the toys and put them on the floor, occasionally glancing at me. I smiled at her. 'Are you OK, love?'

She gave a small nod and looked away.

'Where do you think Lily is?' Peter asked me, looking up from his phone.

'I've really no idea. I haven't seen her since last Thursday when she told me she was going to stay with friends in Newcastle.'

Peter nodded and returned to his phone. When it got to 2.15 I tried calling Lily again. It went through to voicemail, but I didn't leave a message this time. I texted her instead. *Where are you? I'm at the contact centre.*

After five minutes I decided she wasn't going to reply. I began to worry and wondered if she was in hospital, but someone would have contacted me or Eva by now, surely?

At 2.30, with no sign of Lily, Peter stood and went out to reception. I stayed with Olivia, who was still searching the box of toys. She wasn't playing with them as such but was taking them out one at a time and looking at them. How confusing this must all be for her, I thought.

I sat there willing Lily to appear.

Peter returned. 'They're going to call her mobile again. If she doesn't answer, we can go home.'

We waited another five minutes, then the receptionist came into the room. 'I can't get hold of Lily so I suggest you all go. I'll notify the social worker that Lily has missed contact.'

Peter put on Olivia's coat and threw the toys into the box.

'I guess we'll hear from the social worker about Thursday,' he said.

'Yes,' I said quietly. 'I'm so sorry.'

'It's not your fault.'

Yet I felt like it was.

We signed out in reception and in the car park I said goodbye to Olivia. I looked around, half expecting to see

Lily suddenly appear. Now what should I do? I wondered.

I returned to my car and sat in the driver's seat, thinking. I saw Peter drive away, then another car arrived and a woman with a baby got out and went into the centre. The arrangement had been for me to take Lily back home with me today. I tried phoning her mobile again, but it went through to voicemail as before. I didn't leave another message. I thought I should speak to Lily's social worker, so I phoned Eva. Thankfully she was at her desk.

'I know what you are going to say to me,' she said. 'The contact centre has just phoned. I've tried to call Lily's phone, but it's gone to voicemail.'

'I've been trying to phone her for the last hour,' I said. 'I'm still in the car park at present, but I think I'll drive home now.'

'How will Lily get back to you?' Eva asked.

'By train, I suppose. That's how she arrived. She has money to buy a ticket.'

'OK. I'll try her again in about half an hour. Thanks, Cathy.'

I put my phone into the mount on the dashboard and started the car. With a final look around the car park, I drew out and began driving along the road. I was feeling low and wondering what to do. Whatever did Lily think she was playing at, just not turning up? I'd had a wasted trip up here and there was the worry of where Lily could be. Halfway along the road, I suddenly saw her waiting by a hedge. What on earth was she doing there? She saw me and I pulled over and opened the passenger door.

'What's going on?' I asked, hiding my anger. 'Are you coming home with me?'

She nodded and got into the car.

She was dressed in the same clothes she was wearing last Thursday. I waited while she fastened her seat belt, then I began to drive home.

'I need to phone Eva, or you can,' I said.

'You do it.'

She looked worn out and completely exhausted.

I pressed my phone on the dashboard to call Eva.

'Hi, it's Cathy. I've got Lily in the car with me. I found her in the road leading to the centre. I'm driving home now.'

'Thank you. Has she said why she missed contact?'

'No, not yet. I phoned you straight away.'

'Can you put her on, please?'

'We're on hands-free.'

I looked at Lily and eventually she said a subdued 'Hello.'

'Lily, where have you been?' Eva asked evenly.

'I was late for contact, so I thought it was better I didn't go at all.'

'How late?' Eva asked.

'About twenty minutes.'

'You could have still gone in.'

Lily didn't reply.

'I'll speak to you tomorrow when you're home. I need to go now. Thank you, Cathy.'

'Bye,' I said, and ended the call.

There was silence for quite a while, and I knew this was going to be a difficult conversation.

'Are you all right?' I asked her after a few minutes.

'I guess so.'

She certainly didn't look all right. She seemed very lethargic and was slumped back in her seat, gazing out through the windscreen.

'Do you want to talk about it?' I asked.

She shook her head.

I then asked her if she went to the party on Saturday.

'I don't want to talk about it,' she said more firmly, and put in her earpieces.

I noticed they were different earphones to the ones she'd had before, but I didn't comment. I assumed she'd lost the last ones. On the way home she needed to stop off and use the restroom, so I pulled into the next service station. After she'd used the toilet, she bought a large hamburger and chips with a milkshake, which she ate and drank ravenously. I wondered when her last meal was. She then closed her eyes and nodded off. I turned off the radio, and she slept all the way. Not far from home there were some road works and the intermittent stop–start of the car woke her.

'Are we there?' she asked groggily, staring into the dark outside.

'In about ten minutes,' I said. After a few minutes I said. 'Lily, if you want to talk then you know I'm here.'

She nodded.

Five minutes later she suddenly said, 'I'm not sure if I can look after Olivia.'

I looked at her. 'No? What's brought that on?'

'One of the girls where I stayed has a child who is a similar age to Olivia and you've never seen so much work. She couldn't come to the party on Saturday night because of her. In fact, she hasn't been out in the evening since she had her.' I wondered if this was the reason Lily hadn't shown up for contact.

'Parenting is a big responsibility,' I said. 'And it lasts forever.'

'I'm not sure now. I need to think about it.'

'Sleep on it,' I said. 'Then tomorrow, if you are of the same mind, I suggest you talk to Eva.'

We arrived home and Lily went straight to her bedroom and got into bed. Half an hour later, when I went up to check on her, she was fast asleep with most of her clothes still on. I drew the curtains and closed her bedroom door. In the morning, if Lily had made up her mind and still didn't want to parent Olivia, then we needed to tell Eva as soon as possible.

That night I ate with Paula, who'd cooked macaroni cheese. It was absolutely delicious. I didn't tell her what Lily had said. She was busy telling me about a girl she worked with, and had got to know quite well, who had tried to take her own life. It had shocked her deeply, as it had most of the office. She didn't know if or when she would return to work.

That night, Lily had a nightmare. It was the first one she'd had since she'd stayed with me. I woke to her screaming and, throwing on my dressing gown, I rushed round the landing. I gave a quick knock on the door and went in. She was sitting on the edge of the bed, holding her head in her hands and screaming loudly, 'No, don't do that to her!' over and over again.

'Lily,' I said loudly, going to her. 'Lily, you're having a nightmare. Come on, love, wake up.'

She kept screaming and holding her head in her hands, shouting, 'Don't do that to her!' or similar.

Paula appeared at the bedroom door and looked petrified. Her screaming was very loud.

'Lily, come on, you're safe with me. Wake up,' I said repeatedly.

Suddenly she stopped screaming and collapsed against me. I don't think she'd woken at all. She seemed to be asleep on my shoulder. I waited a moment to make sure she was asleep, then Paula helped me tuck her into bed.

'Thanks, love,' I whispered. 'You go back to bed. I'll stay with Lily for a while.'

'Are you sure?' she mouthed.

'Yes.'

She left the bedroom. I sat with Lily and stroked the hair from her forehead as I did with younger children. She seemed to like that. Gradually her face began to relax and eventually she was in a deep and restful sleep. At that moment I felt truly sorry for her. After a while I slowly stood and went back to my bedroom. Eventually I slept.

When Lily came down for breakfast the following morning I asked her how she was.

'I had a shocking nightmare,' she admitted. 'I dreamt that Olivia was being abused as I was.'

'That's dreadful,' I said. 'How awful.' My heart went out to her.

'It was so realistic, and I couldn't get out of the nightmare. You were there too.'

'I heard you scream and came into your room,' I said.

'How embarrassing. I'm sorry,' she said. 'I used to have nightmares a lot, but I haven't had one for a long time.'

She was still clearly shaken by the realism and intensity of the nightmare. It would take a while for it to wear off. Once she'd stopped talking about it, I asked, 'Have you thought any more about what you said yesterday about not parenting Olivia?'

'Yes. I'm still not sure that I want to parent her, but I know I want to see her regularly.'

'So you want her to stay in foster care for now?' I asked.

'I guess so.'

I knew this wasn't fair on Olivia. She was only two and young enough to have a successful adoption. Indeed, she would have been adopted in a few months' time if Lily hadn't reappeared. Eva was phoning today and I hoped she'd talk some sense into Lily. Sometimes we have to act selflessly for the good of our children. If Lily had made up her mind that she didn't want to parent Olivia, then in my view she should be adopted, which would give her a fighting chance of a good life, although I know some would disagree.

CHAPTER TWENTY-SIX

A CALL THAT EVERY CARER DREADS

Eva didn't phone until Wednesday afternoon. I'd tried to call her in the morning, but she was out until after lunchtime. Lily was in the kitchen with her new earphones in when the call came through.

'Eva,' she said, and ran up to her room.

They were talking for a long time. When she came down she said, 'I'm going to see Olivia tomorrow.'

'Good.'

'I told Eva I wanted to see her regularly, but I'm not sure I want to parent her.'

'What did Eva say?' I asked.

'Similar to what you said, that it would mean her staying in foster care. Eva said Olivia was quite young and it would be up to the judge to decide at the final court hearing. But I'm seeing her tomorrow and then I'll stay in Newcastle for the weekend so you can go straight home after contact, and I'll see on Tuesday.'

'Thank you,' I said.

'You don't mind, do you?' she asked.

'I'll do it tomorrow, but if it becomes a regular occurrence then I think you can take the train.'

She looked horrified. 'But I haven't got any money,' she said.

'You had over three hundred pounds last week.'

'I've spent it,' she admitted without a care.

'All of it?' I asked.

'Yes.'

I didn't ask on what.

I thought about what adoption would have meant for Olivia and felt very sad. Now she would be one of over 80,000 children in the UK who were in foster care. I knew it would take the best part of a year for the case to go to court, possibly longer. I assumed that Lily would still visit Olivia twice a week during that time.

That afternoon a few letters arrived; they seemed to come in the afternoon now rather than in the morning. One was addressed to Lily so I handed it to her. It was from the hospital and contained another appointment to see the psychiatrist in a month.

'I'm seeing Olivia on that Tuesday,' she said with immediate satisfaction, 'so I can't go.'

'Phone them and ask for another appointment on a Monday, Wednesday or Friday,' I said.

She stuffed the letter into her pocket and went up to her room. Later, I asked if she'd phoned the hospital. I thought it was important she went to this appointment.

'No, I'll do it tomorrow,' she said nonchalantly.

'Do you want me to get them on the phone, then you can take over?' I asked. I knew they wouldn't speak to me.

'No. I said I'd do it,' she said forcefully.

* * *

The following day was Thursday, so I was up at my usual time. Paula was getting up for work. I fed Sheba, then went upstairs to wake Lily.

'Time to get up. It's Thursday and we're going to see Olivia.'

'I know,' she said groggily. Lily had never been a morning person, so I left her to get dressed in her own time.

Paula went to work and the time ticked by, but there was still no sign of Lily. We needed to leave in half an hour. I couldn't hear her moving around as I made the sandwiches for our lunch in the kitchen, so I went upstairs, knocked firmly on her bedroom door and went in. She was in bed, fast asleep, or at least pretending to be asleep.

'Come on, we're going to contact,' I said.

'I'll get up,' she mumbled.

I left her to get dressed, but downstairs I still couldn't hear her moving around so I went up again. She was still in bed!

'I'm coming,' she moaned. 'Leave me alone.' I waited by the door until she was up.

Eventually, we left the house nearly an hour late. Lily was carrying a large supermarket carrier bag that contained her clothes and make-up. I'd asked her if she wanted a case, but she'd said no.

'Are you all right?' I asked her in the car.

'I guess.' She sighed. 'It's a long way up there and I've been coming here for ages.'

What an odd thing to say about seeing your child at contact, I thought.

'Do you want to go to contact?' I asked her.

She nodded.

I really didn't know what to make of Lily sometimes. She put in her earpieces and, after a small hold-up on the motorway, we arrived at 1.45. I took out the sandwiches and we quickly began eating them. Then a blue Renault Clio pulled up and Eva got out.

'What's she doing here?' Lily demanded, staring at her.

'I think she's going to observe your contact today,' I replied.

'Oh, shit. I don't want her there.'

'Just behave normally,' I said, though I thought that was unlikely to impress Eva.

'I don't want her there,' Lily said again.

'I'm afraid she has a right to observe your contact whenever she chooses. What's the problem?'

Lily didn't answer but threw the rest of her sandwich out of the car window.

Peter's car pulled up and he took Olivia from the rear seat. We got out. Lily wasn't in a good place since she'd seen Eva go into contact.

'Come on, let's go in and say hello to Olivia,' I encouraged.

We went into the contact centre, where Peter was signing the Visitors' Book. Eva was nowhere to be seen. I assumed she'd gone into the contact room or was observing someone else's contact.

I said hello to Olivia and she smiled at me.

'That's a nice smile,' I said as she hid behind Peter's leg.

'How is she settling in?' I asked him as Lily signed the Visitors' Book.

'Slowly. She's often awake at night, calling for her mummy and daddy, and she's very clingy with Angela.'

'That's sad,' I said. 'Hopefully she'll improve with time.'

We went along the corridor towards the contact room. Lily hadn't even said hello to Olivia. We went in and there was the contact supervisor talking to Eva.

'Hello,' Eva said with a welcoming smile. 'Lily, how are you?'

She mumbled something unintelligible.

'I'll see you later,' Peter said, and taking off Olivia's coat left it on a chair.

'I'll wait outside,' I told Eva.

I went out, closed the door and looked back. Lily was standing in the centre of the room and Olivia was standing not far away. Olivia went up to Eva, who said something to Lily, and then I walked away. I could be seen through the glass door. I went down to the waiting room, which was empty. I checked my phone, then picked up some old magazines. I was waiting to see if I could be of any use in contact and also whether Lily wanted to be dropped off somewhere. She'd said she didn't want to go to Tyne and Wear Metro but hadn't said where she wanted to go.

After about half an hour I heard a door open and close and Eva walked past. The door to the waiting room was open and she glanced in.

'I'm off now,' she said to me.

The social worker rarely stayed in contact for the full hour and relied on the contact supervisor's notes.

'Is Lily all right?' I asked her.

She took a step inside the room as she spoke. 'I'm honestly not sure. I'm confused by her sometimes. She's finally playing with Olivia, at least.'

'I think it's very difficult for her.'

'I'm going to suggest a parenting course. It might help her make up her mind whether she wants to parent Olivia or not.'

'That's sounds like a good idea.'

'I understand you are dropping her off and then coming back on Tuesday?'

'Yes. I've said I would.'

'That's very good of you.'

'I feel that some children should have had a better start in life,' I said. 'Lily is one of them.'

'I agree,' Eva said. 'I haven't got any children, but I look after plenty in my job.' She smiled. 'Oh, well, I'd better be off. Bye.'

Unlike most parents who see their children at contact, Lily came out a quarter of an hour early. I wondered if she was ill.

'I've finished,' she said, coming to me in the waiting room.

'But it's only two-forty-five.' Maybe the clock in the room was wrong.

'I know. I've said goodbye to Olivia. I'll tell Peter on the way out.'

I was annoyed, although I didn't say anything then. Leaving Lily by the waiting room door, I went back to the room to check that Olivia was all right. She was standing by the contact supervisor's desk.

'I'll tell Peter to come in if he's in the car park,' I said.

'Thank you.'

I wasn't pleased with Lily. Surely she could have stayed for another quarter of an hour? We quickly signed out of the Visitors' Book and went into the car park. Peter was in his car. He got out when he saw us.

'Is everything all right?' he asked, glancing at Lily.

'Yes. We've finished early today. Olivia is with the supervisor now,' I said.

He looked at Lily, who was texting. 'I guess I'll see you next Tuesday then.'

'I would think so,' I said.

Lily and I began walking to the car.

'Why did you say you *think* so?' Lily demanded.

'Because I'm not sure you'll want to come, given that you've left early today.'

'Of course I'll want to,' she said moodily, and got into the car.

'So why leave contact early?' I asked as I got in beside her.

'Because I'm meeting someone soon.'

I was astounded. She'd left contact early because she was meeting someone!

'Don't ever do that again,' I said. 'Contact takes priority over everything else. Do you understand?'

'I heard you. Can you drop me off at Eldon Square bus station?' she asked.

I sat there for a moment, thinking, then asked her for the postcode, which I put into the sat nav. I was fuming. I didn't know what to say or do. How could I make her understand that she should have stayed at contact for the last quarter of an hour? It was so important, more so than being late to meet someone.

Perhaps she realized she'd annoyed me, for she said, 'We've got to get the bus soon.'

'Who's we?' I asked.

'Me and some friends I met last Saturday.'

'Next time, please arrange to meet them later so you can stay at contact.'

'OK, but I can't today. The bus leaves in half an hour and there isn't another one for two hours. Can we go now?'

I started the car. I could see that Lily hadn't bonded with Olivia, but shouldn't she be working towards it if there was a possibility she might still be able to parent her? I drove in silence following the sat nav's instructions. After about a quarter of an hour it said, 'Take the next turning on the right and you have reached your destination.'

'There they are!' Lily cried as I rounded the corner. 'Bye.'

She picked up her carrier bag, threw open the car door and got out.

'See you on Tuesday,' I called after her.

But she'd already run to join two friends, and they hugged her. I was pleased she was making friends, or possibly renewing old friendships, but her leaving contact early had really got to me. It was only two hours a week, after all.

I pressed home on the sat nav and headed back, my thoughts returning to the fact that Lily hadn't bonded with Olivia or she would never have left contact early. It crossed my mind that perhaps she would rather not have gone to contact today. Was that the reason she was up late? Had she planned to ask me to take her to the bus station instead? I pushed that thought from my mind.

I drove home. Dinner was ready, and after I'd eaten I crashed out on the sofa in front of the television. I was exhausted from the drive.

Two days later, on Saturday morning, I received a phone call that every carer dreads. It was from Lily. She was in hospital in Newcastle, having taken an overdose.

CHAPTER TWENTY-SEVEN

LAST JOURNEY

The call came from Lily's mobile, and she sounded very subdued.

'Cathy, can you come and collect me from the Royal Victoria Infirmary in Newcastle?'

'What are you doing there?' I asked.

She didn't reply.

'Lily, why are you in the Royal Infirmary?'

'I took an overdose last night. They said I can go home now but I need someone to collect me.'

'It will take me at least three hours to get there,' I said.

'I know. I can wait here.'

'Where are you?'

'On the ward. I don't know the name of it. They'll tell you at reception.'

'I'll phone you once I'm there.'

I told Paula where I was going and why.

'I'm so sorry Lily has done that,' she said. 'But why?'

'I don't know yet.'

'I was going out with Liam this afternoon – shall I cancel it?' she asked.

'No, love, you go. There is nothing you can do.'

I smiled and kissed her goodbye.

'Take care,' she said and saw me off at the door.

It was February and the weather was appalling. It rained all the way there, non-stop. Visibility on the motorway was horrendous. I was doing about 40mph for most of the journey, peering through the windscreen at the car in front. I arrived at the hospital at around 4 p.m., exhausted and very worried about Lily. I parked and phoned her.

'Do you want me to come up?' I said.

'No, I'll come down,' she replied.

It appeared they were letting her go without anyone coming to meet her on the ward. I sat in the car, watching the entrance. After about ten minutes Lily appeared. She looked deathly pale and, as she neared the car, I saw there was a large bruise on her cheek.

'Have you got your carrier bag with you?' I asked as she opened the door. I couldn't see it.

'No, I lost it.'

She still had the small bag she'd arrived with over her shoulder and was carrying her phone. I pressed the sat nav and then reversed out of the parking space. Lily sat silently beside me. I didn't know how to begin the conversation. Eventually I said, 'Why did you try to take your own life, Lily?'

'Gary finished with me, but we're OK now. He's phoned me.'

'Who's Gary?' I asked.

'I met him last Saturday, then he finished with me yesterday, but we're back on now. He's got a child he's visiting this weekend, or I would have seen him.'

'You've known him a week?' I checked.

She nodded.

'What tablets did you take?' I asked as I followed the line of traffic.

'Paracetamol. They pumped my stomach at the hospital. It was horrible. I've had it done before.'

I glanced at her. 'When are you seeing Gary next?' I asked.

'I don't know. He's going to let me know, but we're OK now.'

'Does Gary know you have Olivia?' I asked a short while later.

'Yes, of course. I told him when he said he had a kid. He wants his child for some of each week.'

'What I'm not understanding', I said, 'is why you reach for tablets when something goes wrong. It's very dangerous indeed.'

'That's why I do it. It gets a reaction, and fast. It worked this time. Gary is my boyfriend again.'

'But that's emotional blackmail,' I said, shocked, and I looked at her.

She shrugged and continued to scroll through her phone. I knew that Lily's problems were far greater than I could deal with and she needed to see the psychiatrist at our hospital as soon as possible.

'Have you phoned our hospital to rebook your appointment?' I asked her.

'No, but I will.'

'On Monday.'

She didn't reply. There was nothing more I could do. If I phoned the hospital, I knew they wouldn't rebook her appointment without speaking to her, because Lily was eighteen. Today was Saturday and the appointment desk would be closed. I made a mental note for Lily to do it on Monday with me there.

'How many tablets did you take?' I asked, aware it wouldn't have been many. Just enough for her to be able to say she'd taken an overdose and let someone call an ambulance and then get Gary back. Perhaps he'd called the ambulance, I didn't know.

'I don't know, a handful, I guess,' she replied, still looking at her phone.

'It's a dangerous game. One day you will swallow too many and there will be no turning back. It will be the end for you.' I felt I needed to speak forcefully to her to try to make her understand.

'I'm not fussed,' she said casually.

'But why not? You've got a lot going for you, Lily.'

'I'm not fussed,' she said, more loudly than ever, and put her earpieces in.

I concentrated on driving. I felt down that someone with their whole life ahead of them could treat it so carelessly. There are many terminally ill children and teenagers who would give anything to be in Lily's position. It was very upsetting indeed.

Thankfully, the rain had stopped now but it was getting dark. I put the headlights on. I glanced at Lily a few times during the journey, but she had her earpieces in the whole time and was listening to music. I could hear the sound leakage, and I wondered what she was thinking. There'd been no indication of regret, and I thought that when the next hiccup came in her life she could easily take more tablets. She needed to see the psychiatrist quickly.

* * *

We arrived home and the house was empty. Paula was out with Liam. Sheba ran down the hall to greet us, meowing loudly. I stroked her and asked Lily if she wanted something to eat.

'Yes, I'm starving,' she said, having now taken out her earpieces.

I asked her how she had got the bruise on her cheek, but she didn't know. 'I woke up with it,' was all she said, and disappeared up to her room.

I went to the fridge and found a quiche that Paula had made, bless her. I texted her a thank-you and then prepared a salad and warmed French bread to go with it. I called up to Lily's bedroom for her to come down to eat at the table. She arrived straight away with her earpieces in and they remained in during the meal. I didn't comment. Once she'd finished, she went back up to her bedroom. Paula texted, *You're welcome. I'll be home about 11 p.m. Hope everything is all right. x*

I took a cup of tea into the living room. It was now after 9 p.m. I thought of Lily. She had said a few days ago that she didn't want to parent Olivia but wanted to see her regularly. I thought she could change her mind again. Her turbulent lifestyle wasn't really compatible with parenting, and every so often she took an overdose. This was her eighth attempt. Something needed to change in her life before it was too late. I was putting all my hopes on the psychiatrist, who we'd phone on Monday. Would Eva be told about Lily taking this overdose? I wondered. She needed to know, but how would she find out? I doubted the hospital would tell her, so I wondered if I should phone her on Monday to tell her.

As it turned out, Eva phoned Lily.

After I'd asked Lily three times to phone the hospital that Monday morning, she eventually did. They said they would send her another appointment through the post. It was later that day that Lily received the call to her mobile from Eva. She went straight up to her room to take it and was talking for a long time. When she came down she looked as elated as I'd ever seen her.

'I'm going to move to Newcastle,' she declared.

I frowned, puzzled. 'What do you mean?'

'Eva is going to phone around to find me a place and tomorrow I will go straight there after contact. She'll be staying at contact. She told me it's not fair for you to keep driving all the way to Newcastle so she's finding me a bedsit where I can stay. She's going to finalize the arrangements tomorrow morning, but she said I should take all my belongings with me when we go up tomorrow.'

'I see,' I said, both surprised and shocked.

I wasn't sure what I felt. Part of me was happy for Lily, but another part of me said she'd never cope alone.

'I'll be able to see Gary when I want,' she added.

I noticed that seeing Gary had been her first thought, not seeing her daughter.

'I suppose it will be easier for you to see Olivia too,' I added.

'Yes. I'm happy. I'll pack my bags so I'm ready for tomorrow.'

Deep in thought, I took her suitcase from on top of the wardrobe in the third bedroom, together with a smaller holdall, and left her to pack. When Paula came home Lily was in her bedroom as usual, and I told her the news.

'Don't worry. She'll be fine,' she said. 'Lily is a survivor, and you've done your best for her.'

'I know, but I feel we had a way to go yet. I was hoping for a miracle. I guess this is the best outcome, so I'll drive up there tomorrow and come straight back.'

That evening I felt unsettled. After we'd eaten, Lily went to her room to finish her packing. I cleared away, thinking of her. Then I went up to her room.

'Come in,' she called.

'All packed?' I asked her, looking around.

'Yes,' she said with a big smile.

The room looked tidy; everything seemed to be in the case.

'Tomorrow you'll need to put in your toiletries, flannel and toothbrush from the bathroom,' I said.

She nodded and looked at her phone.

I could see it meant nothing to her to be moving – she'd done it so many times before in her life – but it meant something to me. We'd found Lily on the doorstep in the heart of winter and we'd come through a lot together.

'I'll see you in the morning,' I said reluctantly.

'Yes. See you.'

I left her to her phone, came out and closed the door.

That night I lay in bed worrying about Lily's future. I tried to picture her with Olivia, but I couldn't. She just didn't seem to have what it takes to be a mother. But on the other hand, she would have the best part of a year until her case came to court to improve herself, and I sincerely hoped she managed it.

The next morning I woke early and lay there for a while, still thinking of Lily as I had done the night before. I went downstairs, where I could hear Lily moving around above me. I quickly fed Sheba and went upstairs to knock on her bedroom door. She was never awake this early.

'Come in,' she called brightly.

I went in to find her dressed and on her phone. It was 7 a.m.! I was still in my dressing gown. This was the first time I could remember her being up before me.

'You're up early,' I said. 'Do you want breakfast?'

'Yes. Toast. I'll be down shortly.'

When Lily came down I asked her if she'd be able to cook where she was staying, but she had no idea. I suppose it was of little consequence to her as long as she ate something.

'I'll have to forward your mail,' I continued, thinking aloud. 'Text me your address when you know it. You'll have to rebook your hospital appointment at Newcastle. Don't forget, it's important. And tell the universal credit people you have moved. You may get some more money to help you pay for where you're staying. I'll let the solicitor know. You'll need to get one locally.'

Again, I wondered how she was going to get on with all of this.

She took her toast upstairs with her to eat while I showered and dressed. Paula went to Lily's room to say goodbye. I happened to be on the landing and was surprised when Paula was greeted with a big hug from Lily. She wasn't a tactile person.

'Take care,' Paula said. 'I might see you again.'

'No, you won't. There's nothing to bring me back here,' Lily replied with brutal honesty.

'OK. Bye.'

Paula left for work, then at 9.30 a.m. we put Lily's bags and our sandwiches into the car and Lily got in. I returned to the house, checked Lily's bedroom and made sure the bathroom was clear of her belongings. I saw that she'd taken the towels she'd been using. It didn't matter; I had plenty.

I pulled the front door to and joined her in the car.

'All set?' I asked her.

She nodded, so I programmed the sat nav and pulled away. If I thought our last journey together was going to be any different to any other, I was so wrong. She spent the whole time listening to her music or texting Gary. There was the occasional laugh from her. I guess it was something Gary had typed. We arrived at the contact centre a little after 1 p.m.

Lily was too excited to eat her sandwiches, so I put them into a bag for her. She was still texting Gary and laughing every so often as I ate.

'Has Gary got a job?' I asked her after a while.

She shook her head. 'He's looking for one.'

'Where does he live?'

'I'm not sure,' she said, engrossed in her phone.

I gave up and put the radio on, and listened to the news on BBC Radio 4.

Eva arrived at 1.45 and came over to my car.

'Hi,' I said, winding down my window. 'How are you?'

'Good. Have you got Lily's bags with you?' she asked.

'Yes.'

'Lily,' I said, nudging her. She was still texting.

'Yes?' she asked.

'Do you want to put your bags in my car?' Eva asked her. 'Then Cathy can get off.'

We got out of my car and I took the suitcase from the boot and gave the holdall to Lily. We took them to Eva's car.

'Do you know where I'm going yet?' Lily asked her.

'Yes. I'll take you there after contact.'

We put the bags in Eva's car and she locked it. Lily was then heading towards the contact centre, checking her phone as she went.

'Do you want to say goodbye to Cathy?' Eva called after her.

'Oh, yes.'

She stopped where she was and turned.

'Bye, Cathy,' she called.

'Good luck. Give me a ring if you need anything,' I said.

She turned back towards the contact centre. I saw Eva sigh.

'Thank you for everything you've done,' she said to me.

'You're welcome. I'll forward her mail when I have her new address. She needs to book another appointment with a psychiatrist in Newcastle.'

'I'll remind her,' Eva said. 'Thanks again.'

I walked away as they both went into the contact centre. I wanted to say goodbye to Olivia, so I waited in the car park until Peter's black six-seater pulled in.

'Is everything all right?' he asked, seeing me outside as he got out of his car.

'Yes. Lily is moving up here after contact. She's with Eva now inside.'

'I didn't know. I guess it will save you driving here twice a week.'

'Can I just say goodbye to Olivia?'

'Of course.'

He lifted her out of the rear of the car and brought her round to me.

'I don't suppose I'll see you again,' I said to her. 'Bye, love.'

I bent down and kissed her forehead. She didn't say anything but must have known what I was saying, for she suddenly threw her arms around my legs and hugged me hard. Tears sprang to my eyes. I put my hands on her back and gently held her there. Her life had become so unpredictable. It was all about saying goodbye. I stayed where I was for a few minutes with Olivia clutching my legs. Peter smiled.

'She likes you,' he said.

I nodded, then gently eased her away. She looked up at me with big, sorrowful eyes. She knew that I was saying goodbye for good.

'It's been nice knowing you,' Peter said to me, shaking my hand.

'And you.'

'Well, I suppose we'd better go in,' he said.

I was looking at Olivia as he took her hand and began to draw her away. She looked back over her shoulder at me. I swallowed hard and gave a little wave. She kept looking at me as he led her to the front door and pressed the bell. She was still looking at me as it opened and they went in, and then her little face crumpled into tears. That was the last image I had of Olivia, crying, before the door closed.

I went to my car and wept openly. What would happen to her? I wondered. She was young enough to be rescued from the care system, but her naivety wouldn't last much longer. Another year and she would be three – old enough to remember what had happened to her. I sincerely hoped it worked out for her and Lily, honestly I did. Usually, when a teenager leaves my home I have high hopes that they will make a success of it, but not this time. Lily was too wound up in her own life to let it all go for Olivia. I felt it was a disaster waiting to happen and there was nothing I could do to stop it.

I wiped my eyes and pressed *Home* on the sat nav and began to drive. Lily had an hour's contact with Olivia, then Eva would take her to her new home. I vaguely wondered what it was like. She'd said it would be a bedsit.

I arrived home at just gone five o'clock. Paula was still at work. I fed Sheba and then my mobile rang. As I picked it up, to my astonishment I saw that it was Lily.

'Hi, Cathy,' she said, full of the joys of spring. 'I thought I'd phone you just in case Gary tried to contact you.'

'Why should he do that?' I asked. 'I've never met him.'

'No, and you won't. We've finished. Well, I finished with him.'

It was only 5 p.m. and she'd been texting and joking with him all day until I'd left her at 2 p.m.

'All right,' I said. I decided not to ask the reason for the break-up. 'How is your room?'

'Good.'

'And how was Olivia at contact?'

'Fine. I'm going now, but I wanted you to know about Gary.'

And then she was gone, but that was the Lily I was used to. I didn't speak to her again for another few weeks, and then it was in very different circumstances.

CHAPTER TWENTY-EIGHT

AN ACCIDENT

Lily had texted me her new address so I could redirect her mail. I phoned the solicitor and told Mr Stanley's receptionist that Lily had moved and gave her the new address. I also did the same with the hospital and universal credit, although universal credit was already aware – I assumed Lily had told them.

I didn't dislike Lily, but, if I'm honest, I'd found her one of the most – if not *the* most – difficult young person to manage. She wasn't exceptionally naughty, although I'm sure she could have been as a child, but she never truly engaged with me. It was as though there was an invisible brick wall between us. All the other young people I'd fostered had talked to me meaningfully once they'd got to know me, but not Lily. Perhaps if she'd stayed longer, she would have begun to communicate. I was surprised she'd told me about Olivia, although I guessed that was because she needed my help. But even so I wished her well in the future.

Towards the end of March, about a month after Lily had left, I was sitting in the living room one evening, staring through the window. The evenings were lightening now and I hadn't closed the curtains yet. I suddenly thought I'd phone Lily to find out how she was getting on.

'Hello, Cathy,' she said lethargically.

'Hi, Lily, how are you?'

'Not good.'

'What's the matter?'

'I'm in hospital. I took an overdose.' Oh no, I thought, not again. 'They're keeping me in.'

'I'm so sorry,' I said, then my thoughts went to Olivia. 'So you're not seeing Olivia at present?'

'No, I'm not sure I will any more.'

'What's happened?'

'Eva has stopped contact, for now at least. She came to see me yesterday. She said I can see Olivia once I'm better.'

'Do you know how long you're going to be in hospital for?' I asked.

'No, I've been sectioned.'

Being sectioned under the Mental Health Act refers to a person who is detained in a hospital for assessment or treatment due to a mental disorder. This is usually for twenty-eight days to begin with, and you can't just leave.

'I think you're in the best place,' I said. 'Would you like me to visit?'

'I don't mind.' She told me the name of the hospital but didn't know the address.

'I'll find it online. I can come up tomorrow.'

'If you want to,' she said despondently.

'Is there anything you want me to bring?' I asked.

'No. Visiting is 3 p.m. to 8 p.m.'

'I'll get there close to three.'

We said goodbye and I continued to sit there feeling very sad. It had happened again: Lily had taken another overdose. I hoped she now got the treatment she needed.

When Paula arrived home from work I told her I was going to see Lily the following day as she was in hospital. I didn't mention the fact that she'd been sectioned. Paula had her own life to live and didn't need to be worrying about Lily. Paula had suffered with her own mental health during the Covid lockdown, as did many, but she'd bounced back and was fine now, for which I was truly grateful. She had a good job and her relationship with Liam was going well. I wished the same for Lily eventually.

The following day I left home at 9.30 a.m. and stopped off at the supermarket at the end of the High Street. I knew that Lily had said she didn't want anything, but I bought fruit, biscuits, crisps and chocolate, which had all disappeared from our cupboards with regularity when Lily was living with us, so I knew she must like them.

I returned to the car and programmed the sat nav for the hospital in Tyne and Wear. The journey was uneventful; I arrived at 2.30 and parked outside a large stone building, which I knew from what I'd read online had been built in the middle of the nineteenth century. It had a large clock tower and offered a range of psychiatric services. I went in and asked at reception for Lily Saunders, then I followed the directions through a number of doors.

I finally turned left into a room where the door was open. I went in, leaving the door open. It was a small room and Lily was dressed and sitting on the edge of her bed, gazing at her phone. She looked up, saw me and managed a small smile. She looked very pale.

'Hello, love,' I said, going to her. 'How are you?'

'OK,' she said.

'I've brought you a bag of bits and pieces I thought you might fancy.'

I put it on the bed beside her and drew up a chair that was by the wall.

She seemed very low. I looked around the room, which was sparsely furnished with a single bed, a wardrobe and a table.

'How are you doing?' I asked.

I could hear shouting in the distance.

'That's Betty. She's always shouting,' she said.

'Do you need anything?' I asked.

'Not really. Eva brought some toiletries in yesterday. She came to see me.'

'That was nice of her.'

'I'm here for twenty-eight days. I came in a week ago, so there are twenty-one days left.'

I didn't ask what had led to her being sectioned. I thought she'd tell me if she wanted me to know.

'I've been thinking since I've been in here and I don't think I can parent Olivia, but I want to see her sometimes.' She'd said similar before.

'Have you discussed this with Eva?' I asked.

She nodded. 'We talked about it yesterday.'

'What did she say?'

'That I needed to wait and see how I feel when I leave here.' She gave a wide yawn.

I thought she seemed tired; perhaps it was the medication she was undoubtedly taking.

'I would do that then,' I said. 'I'm sure you'll be able to see Olivia again when you leave here.'

She didn't answer but yawned again.

Then a girl who was a similar age to Lily wandered into the room, her long ginger hair floating around her shoulders.

'Hi,' she said languidly. 'I didn't know you had a visitor.' She continued towards Lily's bed.

Lily sprang to life. 'It's OK, you can come and talk to me,' she said.

'Hello,' I said to her. 'I'm Cathy.'

'I'm Clementine, but everyone calls me Clem. Lily is my best friend.' She sat on the bed next to Lily.

'That's nice,' I said. 'Did you two know each other before you came here then?'

'No, we met when we came here,' Clem said, and they both laughed.

Lily seemed far more attentive now. She sat upright on the bed and talked to Clem in a very energetic and lively way. They talked mainly about the people on the ward, who I had no idea of, so I was effectively excluded from the conversation.

I sat there listening for a while, occasionally nodding, but their talk seemed very intrusive and, if I'm honest, not nice. We all have our problems. I guessed it was because they were young. After about ten minutes or so I said, 'Shall I go then?'

'OK,' Lily said easily and continued talking to Clementine.

'Bye,' I said, and stood.

Neither of them so much as looked at me. I put the chair back where I'd found it and said goodbye again. It fell on deaf ears.

I left them chatting enthusiastically about the meals at

the hospital – apparently dinner was the worst. As I walked away I glanced at my watch. I'd been inside for under half an hour. I doubted I'd visit again. It was a long drive, and I wasn't sure Lily wanted me there.

I got into my car and drove home, wondering if I'd hear any more from Lily.

A week passed and I decided to start phoning her once a week to see how she was. I worried about her. They were short calls and when I asked her how she was doing she said 'OK' or 'fine' or similar. Sometimes she sounded down and at other times quite elated. She was in the hospital for more than twenty-eight days, but then one week when I phoned her she said, 'I'm out of here next week.'

'That's good. Are you going back to your bedsit?' I asked.

'I'm not sure yet.'

'Where else would you go?'

'I don't know.'

'There's always a bed here for you,' I said.

'Oh, no. That's not necessary.'

So I decided that Eva was in charge and would make any arrangements required for her.

A few days after Lily's discharge, Eva phoned me. It was late afternoon, and I was in the living room using my laptop.

'Sorry to bother you, Cathy, but do you know where Lily is? She was discharged from hospital the day before yesterday, but when I went to the hospital to collect her she'd already gone. I can't get hold of her. I've tried phoning.'

'No, I'm sorry. How very worrying. She hasn't been in touch with me. Has she not gone back to the accommodation you found her?'

'She went to her room when she was discharged and collected some of her belongings but then left.'

'She hasn't been in touch with me,' I said. 'I spoke to her last week on the phone and she said she wasn't sure where she was going.'

'Will you tell me if she gets in touch with you?' Eva asked.

'Yes, of course. I do hope you find her.'

I ended the call and straight away phoned Lily's mobile. It rang and rang but she didn't pick up. She would know it was me calling, just as she would have when it was Eva. I hoped she was all right and not in hospital again. I decided to text her.

Are you OK? Eva just phoned. She's looking for you, I wrote.

Half an hour later my mobile sounded with a text message. It was from Lily.

In Itali with Clem. Havin a gr8 time out heer.

Struth! So she was safe and travelling, like many young people do.

I messaged back: *Have a lovely time. When will you return?*

She replied: *Mite not com back. It's gr8 heer and we've mett Marco and Andrea.*

Take care, I replied.

I telephoned Eva. She was in a meeting, so I left a message for her to call me when she came out. Half an hour later she phoned.

'I've had a text message from Lily saying she's travelling in Italy,' I said.

'Really? How did she get there?' Eva asked, as surprised as I was by this revelation.

'I don't know but she's with a friend from the hospital. I met her briefly when I visited. She's called Clem. I don't know her surname.'

'I see. Do you know when she's planning on returning?'

'When I asked her she said she might not come back, but that's Lily. It could mean soon or never. There's not much to keep her here,' I added.

'Apart from Olivia.'

'How is she?' I asked.

'She's settling down now without the twice-weekly contact, although I think she's struggling with the three boys. But she's always pleased to see me.'

'That's nice.'

'Cathy …' Eva said, as though she was going to ask me something.

'Yes?'

'It doesn't matter. I'll sort it out.'

'Sure?'

'Yes. Thanks again. If Lily shows up or gets in touch, please let me know.'

'I will.'

I vaguely wondered what Eva was going to say when she sounded as though she was going to ask me a question, but then my phone rang again. It was Kirsty.

'Hi, Cathy. How are you?'

'Good. And you?'

'Yes, fine,' she said in a hurry. 'Can we use your name for our fostering application, please?'

'Yes, of course. How's it going?'

'There's a lot of paperwork to do. I'm tackling some of it now.'

'I won't keep you then. See you soon.'

I knew how precious time was when you had a job and a young child.

Their social worker, Delia Thomas, phoned me the next day to make an appointment to visit.

'I'm guessing you know what it's about,' she said.

'Adrian and Kirsty's application to foster.'

'That's correct.'

She came at 4 p.m. the day after that. I knew roughly what to expect. Of course, I hoovered the house from top to bottom before her arrival. Who wouldn't?

When she arrived I made her a coffee while she stroked Sheba and told me about her cats. Then she opened her laptop and asked me how long I'd known Kirsty. I told her since Adrian had started dating her at university. She said she wasn't going to ask me about my son as I would be prejudiced in his favour, but she asked me how I viewed Kirsty.

'She's a really nice person,' I said. 'We've never fallen out in all these years, and there's not many who can say that. They have a daughter, Sophia, who is my granddaughter. She's lovely.'

'I've met her,' Delia said.

'She is one of my three grandchildren. Lucy and Darren have the other two.'

'Yes, I'm going to visit them next week. How strong is Adrian and Kirsty's relationship?' She was reading off a checklist on her laptop.

'It's very strong. Unlike mine was,' I said.

'Can you tell me a bit about why you and your husband separated?' she asked.

'He met a younger woman from his office. My children used to see him regularly and know they still can, but now they are older they choose not to.'

'Thank you.' I waited while she typed.

'How much of a part did Adrian and Kirsty play when you fostered full-time?' she asked.

'They see us regularly, about every two weeks. Kirsty always played or interacted with the child as part of our family, just as Adrian did.'

She typed as I spoke.

'And negative? What would you say about Kirsty's failings?'

I thought for a while and tried to think of something I could say. Delia's fingers hovered over the keys. Then she took a sip of her tea.

'I honestly can't think of anything,' I said at last. 'She's a lovely person and Adrian is a very lucky guy to have her.'

She laughed and then typed. 'I'll write none.'

The next questions were about their financial situation, and I told her what I knew. 'Have they ever got into financial hardship?' she asked.

'Not that I'm aware of. I've told them to ask me if they do. I know they are doing up their house, which costs a lot.'

'Yes, it looks nice. Kirsty and Adrian have applied to foster under-fives. Do you think that will work?' she asked, taking another sip of her tea.

'I think so. Kirsty is a teacher, but I know she is hoping to work part-time or do supply in future.'

'And you are going to be their nominated carer, I believe?'

'That's right.'

A nominated carer is someone who provides support care for the applicants. They have been assessed and approved and can either provide the care in the foster carer's home or their own. It is usually when the main carer is ill or they have to go to a meeting, for example.

The front door opened as Paula came home from work. I introduced her to Delia.

'Have you got time to answer a couple of questions?' Delia asked her.

'Yes,' Paula said, sitting self-consciously in a chair.

'How do you get on with your brother and sister-in-law?'

'Very well. I always have. I think they'll make excellent foster parents.'

'Are you going to help look after the child?' she asked.

'Yes, with my mother.'

'Any plans to foster in the future?' she asked.

Paula looked horrified. 'No.'

'You may change your mind in years to come,' she said with a smile as she typed.

She asked Paula how her job was going, then said she could go if she wished. She went upstairs to change while we talked about other aspects of fostering. After about two hours, Delia thanked me and left. I immediately phoned Kirsty and told her I thought it had gone very well.

'I've been thinking of you all afternoon,' she said. 'Thank you so much.'

Later that evening I was sitting in the living room, while Paula was upstairs. We'd eaten and I now had a cup of tea at my side. My mobile rang, and as I picked it up I saw it was Angela. For a moment I couldn't think who Angela was, then I suddenly thought of Olivia and answered the call. I was right.

'Have you got a minute?' she asked. She sounded very flustered and unnerved.

'Yes. What is it?'

'There's been an accident – I'm with Olivia in the hospital. Peter is at home with the boys. What's Lily's number? I know I need to phone the parents.'

I could feel my heart rate start to rise.

'What's happened?' I asked.

'She's broken her arm. Jackson, the last boy to arrive with us, jumped off the sofa onto her.'

'Oh, no.'

'It would happen now, after all these years!' she said. 'She is too precious. They should have given us another boy. What's Lily's number?'

'Have you contacted the social services?' I asked.

'I'll do that next.'

'I would do it now. It'll be the out-of-hours team on duty as it's so late.'

'Yes, yes, I know.'

I knew how serious the repercussions of this could be.

'It was an accident waiting to happen,' Angela said. 'The kid was in agony when I brought her here.'

'I'm so sorry. Please phone the social services now. I'm sure they will try to speak to Lily. I'll phone you tomorrow to see how Olivia is.'

The poor woman was in a right state alone at the hospital. I wondered if Olivia had been one child too many for them to foster, even with two parents. Four was a lot. I knew there was a shortage of foster carers, and perhaps Olivia wouldn't have been placed with Angela and Peter in different circumstances. You have to be so careful when fostering and treat the child with even more care than you would your own. I hoped Olivia was all right.

CHAPTER TWENTY-NINE

EVA AND HER MOTHER

The following day I phoned Angela and she said that Olivia was home now with her arm in plaster. She sounded calmer. Eva had been notified, and she was visiting their home later today.

'Did you have to phone Lily?' I asked.

'No, the social services were going to do that. Do you want to speak to Olivia?' she asked. 'It might help cheer her up.'

'Yes, that would be nice.'

She put her on the phone and I heard Angela encouraging her. 'Say hello to Cathy.'

A small voice came through. 'Hello,' she said.

'Hi, love, how are you? I hear you have a sore arm.'

'Yes,' she said. 'It's bad.'

Olivia's language had come on a lot since I'd last seen her.

'I'm sure it will get better soon,' I said.

'Yes. Bye,' she said, suddenly ending the call as children that age do.

'Bye, love,' I said.

Angela came back on the call.

'I've just heard the front door go. I think that could be Eva.'

'Bye, then.'

I thought about Angela, Peter and Eva for the rest of the day. I knew there would be negative outcomes and I hoped they weren't too bad, but it's a major incident when a child comes to harm while in the care of a foster carer, as had happened here. I wondered how Lily would take it. Would she fly straight back to her daughter? I assumed so.

When Paula arrived home that night she said the girl in her office who'd tried to take her own life was back at work now, looking better than she had done in a long while. Paula and some of the others in the office were going out of their way to talk to her. I was pleased. Sometimes people with mental health issues are shunned.

I waited another week, then phoned Angela to see how Olivia was doing.

'She's not here,' she said stoically. 'She was removed by Eva. It's probably for the best.'

'I'm sorry. Where is she now? Do you know?'

'I don't know. The social worker came and took her.'

'Do you know if Lily was informed?'

'No. But the social services had a meeting the day after Olivia broke her arm and decided that four children, including three boys, was the main reason for the accident. They took Olivia the next day. As I said, it's probably for the best.'

'Yes,' I agreed half-heartedly, for it meant another move for Olivia and all that would entail.

Suddenly, I heard a loud crash in the background, followed by Peter's loud and angry voice.

'What the hell!' Angela exclaimed.

'I'll leave you to it,' I said. 'Will you be getting any more children?'

'We are still approved for four, but I think it will be an older child, probably a boy, who can stick up for themselves.'

There was another loud crash with more shouting, so we said goodbye.

I thought about Olivia going to another home. How would she cope? The poor child. The carer would likely have more than one child and Olivia was probably young enough to share a bedroom. My thoughts worked overtime as I imagined how upset she was going to be. This would be her third home in four months. I really wanted to talk to Olivia, just to make sure she was all right. Mine would at least be a familiar voice, as well as Eva's.

I waited a few days, then I telephoned Eva.

'She's got this week off,' a colleague told me.

'I'll phone back. It's nothing urgent,' I said.

The following Monday was a sunny day in late April. The sun had some real warmth in it and the sky was bright blue. It made me happy. All the birds were chirping and nesting, and the garden had suddenly come alive. The air was fresh and I thought we had a hedgehog in the garden as I could see traces that it left behind. I put out a bowl of fresh water, did some gardening, then came indoors. Eva would have returned to work by now. I waited until the afternoon and phoned her.

'Hello, Cathy,' she said brightly. 'How are you?'

'Fine. How are you?'

'Good.'

'I was wondering where Olivia was now. I'd like to phone her if possible, just to say hello. I'm aware that she's left Angela and Peter's.'

There was a short pause before she said, 'Yes, she did. She's with me.'

I thought I'd misheard her, then she continued. 'After we removed her from Angela and Peter's, I brought her to live with my mother and me. Did you know we were foster carers?'

I swallowed a tear. This was the best possible outcome for Olivia I could imagine – to be fostered by Eva and her mother.

'That's incredible,' I said. 'Thank goodness. I didn't know you fostered. Will she stay with you?'

'Yes. It's early days yet but I'm planning on applying to the court for a Special Guardianship Order, then Lily will be able to see her regularly, but she won't be able to remove her without a court order.'

My eyes filled. 'I'm so pleased,' I said. 'How is she in herself?'

'She's doing all right. She's been with me over a week now and is slowly settling in. Mum is great with her. Thankfully, our last child left the week before. I hadn't planned on having another one straight away, but when we decided that Olivia couldn't stay where she was she came to me. A colleague of mine suggested it.'

'I'm truly pleased,' I said. 'What a great outcome! I needn't worry about her any more now she's with you and your mother.'

A tear escaped and ran down my cheek.

'Why don't you come and visit us? If it's not too far. Give it a few weeks, then come and say hi if you like. I'm sure Olivia will remember you. She remembers the book.'

'What book?' I asked.

'The one about the animals. You remember, you used to read it to her at contact and make the noises – *ribbit, ribbit, oink, oink*.'

'Oh, no,' I said with a laugh. 'She doesn't remember that, does she?'

'She certainly does. You'd be surprised what a child of that age remembers, especially the bad things.'

'I know. What about Lily? Has she seen Olivia?'

'No, although I've spoken to her on the phone a few times. She's still in Italy with her friend Clem and two lads. I've explained my plans for Olivia and reassured her that she'll be safe and is doing well. I think that underneath it all she is relieved that I'm looking after her.'

'I'm sure she is. What an outcome! I still can't believe it. So she will stay with you until she's eighteen?'

'I hope she'll be with us forever. She already feels like our daughter.'

'Wonderful,' I said through my tears. 'I'll give you a ring to arrange a visit in a few weeks.'

CHAPTER THIRTY

SAYING GOODBYE

It was a lovely day in the middle of May. I'd texted Eva to arrange to visit her on Sunday and she'd sent me her address. Paula was out for the day with Liam. I decided, rather than make some sandwiches, that I'd stop at a motorway service station for a late lunch on the way back. I was due there about midday but Eva had said to come in as soon as I arrived.

It was a good journey with not too much traffic as it was a Sunday. I had BBC Radio 4 on for most of the way. I arrived outside her house in a village on the outskirts of Newcastle at 11.45 a.m. I was just checking I had the right address when the front door opened and there stood Eva and Olivia with her arm in plaster. I guessed they'd been watching out for me. I immediately got out of the car, smiling.

'Hi! How are you?' I called.

'We're all good,' Eva said. 'Come in.'

I walked up the path and gave the bunch of flowers I'd brought with me to Eva and said hi to Olivia.

'Thank you so much. That's nice of you. They're beautiful,' Eva said.

I looked at Olivia as we went in. Her large round eyes were examining me quizzically and she was holding on to Eva's leg.

'How are you all?' I asked.

'OK. Olivia is a bit shy at present,' Eva said. 'These flowers are beautiful. Look, Olivia.' She showed her the blooms.

We turned left into the one main room that ran from the front of the house to the back. It was a lovely old terraced house that had been renovated. There were sash windows at either end, making the room very light. A lady had just risen from the sofa.

'This is my mother, Teresa,' Eva said, introducing her.

'Hi, how are you?' I went over to her.

'Very good, thank you.'

Olivia ran to Teresa, while Eva went into the kitchen to put the flowers in a vase.

'She'll thaw out soon,' Teresa said, referring to Olivia, who clung to her.

'I'm sure she will.'

'I think it's a bit hot to go into the garden,' Teresa said, looking at me.

'Whatever you want to do,' I said.

I offered the present I had in my bag to Olivia, who was now sitting on Teresa's lap.

'Say thank you to Cathy,' Teresa said.

'Thank you,' Olivia said.

'Good girl. I hear you're a foster carer too?' Teresa said to me.

'Yes, I used to foster full time.'

'We've been fostering for ten years. We began after Laurence died. He was Eva's husband. I was living alone at the time, so it made sense for me to move in with her. I enjoy fostering very much. Did you?'

'Yes. I still do respite fostering now,' I said. 'I think once you start it's difficult to stop.'

'Absolutely!' Teresa laughed.

Olivia had stopped clutching the present I'd bought her and was now busy unwrapping it. Eva came in and set the vase of flowers on the main table behind us.

'They're really beautiful,' she said. 'I've made us a bit of lunch. Are you ready to eat?'

'I'm always ready for lunch,' Teresa said with a smile, and she looked at me.

'That's nice of you. Yes, please,' I said.

Eva disappeared back into the kitchen and presently brought out salmon parcels with a bowl of mixed salad and set them on the large coffee table in front of us.

'We'll eat in here,' she said.

'That looks lovely,' I said.

Olivia had succeeded in unwrapping the present I'd bought for her, which was a beautifully illustrated book on animals.

'That's a nice present,' Teresa said. 'She likes animals, don't you?'

Olivia looked at me and nodded. She still wasn't sure of me.

Eva brought out a tray of tea and Olivia went and sat at the small children's table to one side. Eva took one of the salmon parcels and put it on a child's plate, then cut it up into manageable pieces. She did the same with the salad. Oliva began to eat with her good hand.

'She has her plaster off next week,' Teresa said.

'That'll feel a lot better,' I said.

I helped myself to the salmon parcels and salad.

'She's very quiet,' Eva said, also helping herself as her mother was doing. 'I wonder what she's thinking.'

'She's probably wondering, who is this strange woman?' I said, referring to myself.

Eva smiled. 'I think she's still very wary of new people coming into the house.'

'With good reason,' Teresa added.

'I've just come for a visit,' I told Olivia. 'Then I'm going home alone.'

'Are you going to speak to Cathy?' Teresa asked her.

'Hi,' Olivia said, looking bashful.

Partway through the meal, she suddenly stood and went to the small bookshelf against one wall and took out a book. She brought it over and placed it on my lap. 'Finish your lunch,' Teresa told her.

I set my plate to one side and looked at the book. Olivia was still waiting there next to me, so I lifted her onto my lap. It wasn't until I opened the book that I realized it was the same one about animals that I'd read to her at contact. Eva had bought a copy for her.

I gave her a hug.

As I read the book and made the noises – '*Ribbit, ribbit. Oink, oink. Neigh, neigh. Moo*' – my eyes glazed over. How different Olivia's life was now, I thought.

Her little face lost its serious expression and she began to smile.

'*Ribbit, ribbit*,' she said, and gave a laugh.

'That's right. *Oink, oink*,' I said.

I read the book, and then she wanted me to read it again, which I did – this time without any tears. Then she said, 'Go in my garden,' as clearly as anything.

'When we've finished eating,' Teresa replied.

We'd finished our lunch, then Eva took the plates into the kitchen as Teresa, Olivia and I went out through the patio doors into the back garden. It was a lovely cottage-style garden with tall hollyhocks, roses, foxgloves, phlox and many more plants, all competing for space in this tiny garden. I admired it. It put my garden to shame.

Eva came out and explained that it was her mother's domain; she loved gardening. Teresa was a similar age to me, and we chatted for a while about the plants as Eva played with Olivia. After a while Teresa said, 'It's very hot out here. Shall we go inside?'

'I think so,' Eva said.

'I need to be going before long,' I said, once we were indoors. 'I've got a three-hour drive back.'

The air was much cooler inside. Olivia was holding Teresa's hand once again.

'Bye, Cathy,' Olivia said spontaneously.

'That's lovely,' Eva said. 'Say thank you for your present.'

'Thank you,' she said, and smiled sheepishly.

She seemed a lot happier now I was going but was still holding Teresa's hand tightly. We went towards the front door and then, without being asked or prompted, and perhaps sensing there was no danger, she dropped Teresa's hand and came to me with her lips pursed ready for a kiss. I lowered my cheek and she kissed it so delicately.

'Thank you,' I smiled. 'That was lovely.' My eyes misted over.

The three of them stood on the front doorstep and watched me get into the car. I lowered the windows.

They waited while I programmed the sat nav, ready to set off for home.

'Come again if you are passing!' Eva called.

'I will do.'

I waved as I drove away. It was the best family that Olivia could have wished for, and I was truly pleased. I knew she would make them as happy as they would make her.

Six months later, Eva phoned.

'Hi,' she said. 'How are you?'

'Good.'

'Sorry to trouble you, but have you heard from Lily?'

'No.'

'I'm preparing the paperwork for court for the Special Guardianship Order and I can't get hold of her. Can you text her and tell her I need to speak to her? She replies to your texts.'

'Sure. How is Olivia?'

'She's doing very well. Do you know what her favourite book is?'

I thought for a moment, then said, '*Ribbit, ribbit. Oink, oink?*'

'Exactly.'

We both laughed, then we chatted for a while. Once we'd finished talking, I messaged Lily straight away, using the last number I had for her.

Can you contact Eva? She is going to apply for special guardianship and needs to talk to you.

She replied straight away. *Yh, sure. Hru? We're stil in Itali havin a gr8 time.*

I messaged Eva and told her of Lily's response. I assumed she'd got in touch with Eva, as six months later Eva texted me to say that the Special Guardianship Order had been granted to her. Lily hadn't seen her daughter at all, but when she returns to this country she can. I couldn't have wished for a better outcome, and I was truly grateful.

SUGGESTED TOPICS FOR READING-GROUP DISCUSSION

Cathy finds Lily on her doorstep on Boxing Day night and she stays. Would you have allowed her to stay indefinitely, knowing so little about her and without access to her social services files?

Lily has a clear recollection of staying with Cathy ten years before. How far back can you clearly remember?

How would you describe Lily's personality?

Does Cathy always deal with Lily's behaviour in an acceptable way? Give some examples.

What are the pros and cons of permanency fostering?

What are the contrasts between Paula's and Lily's personalities?

Is attempting to take her own life a cry for help from Lily, as is suggested in the book? What evidence is there for this?

I was surprised by the statistic at the start of the book, that suicide accounts for 1 per cent of deaths globally. What is your view?

CHRONOLOGY

If you would like to read, or re-read, my books in chronological order, here is the list to date:

Cut
The Silent Cry
Daddy's Little Princess
Nobody's Son
Cruel to be Kind
The Night the Angels Came
A Long Way from Home
A Baby's Cry
The Saddest Girl in the World
Please Don't Take My Baby
Will You Love Me?
I Miss Mummy
Saving Danny
Girl Alone
Where Has Mummy Gone?
Damaged
Hidden
Mummy Told Me Not to Tell
Another Forgotten Child
The Child Bride
Can I Let You Go?
Finding Stevie
Innocent
Too Scared to Tell
A Terrible Secret
A Life Lost
An Innocent Baby
Neglected
A Family Torn Apart
Unwanted
Unsafe
Helpless
No One to Miss Me

The titles below can be slotted in anywhere, as can my Lisa Stone thrillers: http://lisastonebooks.co.uk/:

The Girl in the Mirror
My Dad's a Policeman
Run, Mummy, Run
Happy Kids
Happy Adults
Happy Mealtimes for Kids
About Writing and How to Publish

This list is also on the books page of my website: https://cathyglass.co.uk/true-stories-cathy-glass/

Cathy Glass

One remarkable woman, more than **150** foster children cared for.

Cathy Glass has been a foster carer for 30 years, during which time she has looked after more than 150 children, as well as raising three children of her own. She was awarded a degree in education and psychology as a mature student, and writes under a pseudonym. To find out more about Cathy and her story visit **www.cathyglass.co.uk**.

Helpless

Riley and his two little siblings, Jayden and Lola, are not safe at home

With all three children in her care, will Cathy be able to rebuild their lives – and their mother Janie's?

Unsafe

Damian longs for home and, with Cathy's help, is overcoming his many issues and nearing a return

But when his mother's new boyfriend arrives, Cathy becomes deeply concerned.

Unwanted

Lara was seven when she was put into foster care after her mother died from a drug overdose

The care system failed Lara and now she is failing her son . . .

A Family Torn Apart

Angie and Polly are loved and looked-after by their parents, so why are they brought into foster care?

But as they settle with Cathy, and start to talk of life at home, it becomes clear something is badly wrong.

Neglected

The police remove Jamey from home as an emergency and take him to foster carer Cathy

But as Jamey starts to settle in and make progress a new threat emerges, which changes everything.

An Innocent Baby

Abandoned at birth, Darcy-May is brought to Cathy with a police escort

Her teenage mother wants nothing to do with her, but why? She is an adorable baby.

A Life Lost

Jackson is aggressive, confrontational and often volatile

Then, in a dramatic turn of events, the true reason for Jackson's behaviour comes to light . . .

A Terrible Secret

Tilly is so frightened of her stepfather, Dave, that she asks to go into foster care

The more Cathy learns about Dave's behaviour, the more worried she becomes ...

Too Scared to Tell

Oskar has been arriving at school hungry, unkempt and bruised. His mother has gone abroad and left him in the care of 'friends'

As the weeks pass, Cathy's concerns deepen. Oskar is clearly frightened of someone – but who? And why?

Innocent

Siblings Molly and Kit arrive at Cathy's frightened, injured and ill

The parents say they are not to blame. Could the social services have got it wrong?

Finding Stevie

Fourteen-year-old Stevie is exploring his gender identity

Like many young people, he spends time online, but Cathy is shocked when she learns his terrible secret.

Where Has Mummy Gone?

When Melody is taken into care, she fears her mother won't cope alone

It is only when Melody's mother vanishes that what has really been going on at home comes to light.

A Long Way from Home

Abandoned in an orphanage, Anna's future looks bleak until she is adopted

Anna's new parents love her, so why does she end up in foster care?

Cruel to be Kind

Max is shockingly overweight and struggles to make friends

Cathy faces a challenge to help this unhappy boy.

Nobody's Son

Born in prison and brought up in care, Alex has only ever known rejection

He is longing for a family of his own, but again the system fails him.

Can I Let You Go?

Faye is 24, pregnant and has learning difficulties as a result of her mother's alcoholism

Can Cathy help Faye learn enough to parent her child?

The Silent Cry

A mother battling depression. A family in denial

Cathy is desperate to help before something terrible happens.

Girl Alone

An angry, traumatized young girl on a path to self-destruction

Can Cathy discover the truth behind Joss's dangerous behaviour before it's too late?

Saving Danny

Danny's parents can no longer cope with his challenging behaviour

Calling on all her expertise, Cathy discovers a frightened little boy who just wants to be loved.

The Child Bride

A girl blamed and abused for dishonouring her community

Cathy discovers the devastating truth.

Daddy's Little Princess

A sweet-natured girl with a complicated past

Cathy picks up the pieces after events take a dramatic turn.

Will You Love Me?

A broken child desperate for a loving home

The true story of Cathy's adopted daughter Lucy.

Please Don't Take My Baby

Seventeen-year-old Jade is pregnant, homeless and alone

Cathy has room in her heart for two.

Another Forgotten Child

Eight-year-old Aimee was on the child-protection register at birth

Cathy is determined to give her the happy home she deserves.

A Baby's Cry

A newborn, only hours old, taken into care

Cathy protects tiny Harrison from the potentially fatal secrets that surround his existence.

The Night the Angels Came

A little boy on the brink of bereavement

Cathy and her family make sure Michael is never alone.

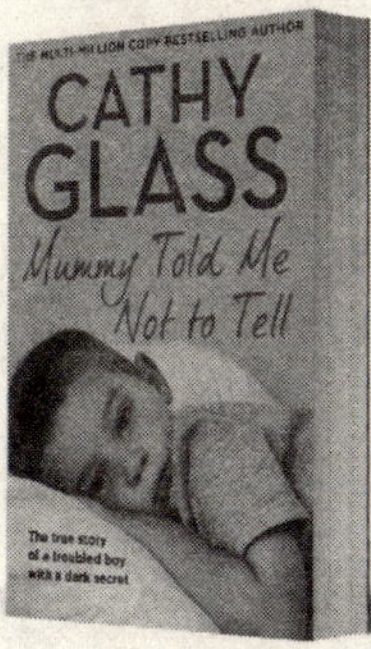

Mummy Told Me Not to Tell

A troubled boy sworn to secrecy

After his dark past has been revealed, Cathy helps Reece to rebuild his life.

I Miss Mummy

Four-year-old Alice doesn't understand why she's in care

Cathy fights for her to have the happy home she deserves.

The Saddest Girl in the World

A haunted child who refuses to speak

Do Donna's scars run too deep for Cathy to help?

Cut

Dawn is desperate to be loved

Abused and abandoned, this vulnerable child pushes Cathy and her family to their limits.

Hidden

The boy with no past

Can Cathy help Tayo to feel like he belongs again?

Damaged

A forgotten child

Cathy is Jodie's last hope. For the first time, this abused young girl has found someone she can trust.

Run, Mummy, Run

The gripping story of a woman caught in a horrific cycle of abuse, and the desperate measures she must take to escape.

My Dad's a Policeman

The dramatic short story about a young boy's desperate bid to keep his family together.

The Girl in the Mirror

Trying to piece together her past, Mandy uncovers a dreadful family secret that has been blanked from her memory for years.

About Writing and How to Publish

A clear, concise practical guide on writing and the best ways to get published.

Happy Mealtimes for Kids

A guide to healthy eating with simple recipes that children love.

Happy Adults

A practical guide to achieving lasting happiness, contentment and success. The essential manual for getting the best out of life.

Happy Kids

A clear and concise guide to raising confident, well-behaved and happy children.

CATHY GLASS WRITING AS

LISA STONE

www.lisastonebooks.co.uk

The new crime thrillers that will chill you to the bone . . .

THE FOREVER HOUSE

What if your forever home became your worst nightmare?

THE MURDER ROOM

Your house should be the safest place in the world. Shouldn't it?

THE GATHERING

Can old friends still be trusted?

THE COTTAGE

Is someone out there?

TAKEN

Have you seen Leila?

THE DOCTOR

How much do you know about the couple next door?

STALKER

Security cameras are there to keep us safe. Aren't they?

THE DARKNESS WITHIN

You know your son better than anyone. Don't you?

Be amazed
Be moved
Be inspired

Follow Cathy:

/cathy.glass.180

@CathyGlassUK

www.cathyglass.co.uk

Cathy loves to hear from readers and reads and replies to posts, but she asks that no plot spoilers are posted, please. We're sure you appreciate why.